PERCUSSION DISCOGRAPHY

**Recent Titles in
Discographies**

The Cliff Edwards Discography
Larry F. Kiner, compiler

Broadway on Record: A Directory of New York Cast Recordings of Musical Shows,
1931-1986
Richard Chigley Lynch, compiler

The Blue Note Label: A Discography
Michael Cuscuna and Michel Ruppli, compilers

His Master's Voice/La Voce Del Padrone
Alan Kelly, compiler

Irish Folk Music: A Selected Discography
Deborah L. Schaeffer, compiler

Movie Musicals On Record: A Directory of Recordings of Motion
Picture Musicals, 1927-1987
Richard Chigley Lynch, compiler

Classical Music Discographies, 1976-1988: A Bibliography
Michael Gray, compiler

You Got To Be Original, Man! The Music of Lester Young
Frank Büchmann-Møller

The Decca Hillbilly Discography
Cary Ginell, compiler

PERCUSSION DISCOGRAPHY

An International Compilation
of Solo and Chamber Percussion Music

Compiled by
Fernando A. Meza

Discographies, Number 36

Greenwood Press
New York • Westport, Connecticut • London

REF.
ML
156.4
P4
M617
1990
c.1

Library of Congress Cataloging-in-Publication Data

Meza, Fernando A.
   Percussion discography : an international compilation of solo and
chamber percussion music / compiled by Fernando A. Meza.
      p.   cm.—(Discographies, ISSN 0192-334X ; no. 36)
   ISBN 0-313-26867-3 (lib. bdg. : alk. paper)
      1. Percussion music—Discography.   2. Percussion ensembles—
Discography.   I. Title.   II. Series.
   ML156.4.P4M5   1990
   016.7868 '026 '6—dc20   89-28647

British Library Cataloguing in Publication Data is available.

Library of Congress Catalog Card Number: 89-28647
ISBN: 0-313-26867-3
ISSN: 0192-334X

First published in 1990

Greenwood Press, 88 Post Road West, Westport, CT   06881
An imprint of Greenwood Publishing Group, Inc.

Printed in the United States of America

The paper used in this book complies with the
Permanent Paper Standard issued by the National
Information Standards Organization (Z39.48-1984).

10 9 8 7 6 5 4 3 2 1

Contents

Preface

The need for a discography of percussion has now been around for quite some time. Since the recording industry, the composers, and the performers of percussion instruments have collaborated in creating quality recordings, this need has been obvious in terms of further disseminating the extensive world of percussion literature. It is my hope that this book will help in such effort in two ways: First, by guiding those who already know or are interested in knowing more about a particular piece of music to the correct source of where to obtain an actual sound recording, and second, by creating an interest in those who do not yet know, but who would like to experience the wonderful sounds and creative spirits of some of the twentieth century's most remarkable composers, arrangers, and performers.

The main purpose of this book is to provide the reader with information about recordings (LP's, CD's, or cassettes) in which percussion instruments are featured as solo instruments (i.e., marimba, timpani, multiple percussion, etc.) or as part of a chamber ensemble (i.e., percussion ensemble, or in combination with other instruments-vibraphone and flute; saxophone and percussion; piano, percussion, and electronic sounds, etc.). The book is organized alphabetically by the composer's last name, and within each composer's output, by the title of the composition. The record company and the recording catalog number are given immediately following, and when possible, the performer(s) name has been provided at the last line of each entry.

Therefore, the information will comply with the following format:

COMPOSER'S NAME (and dates when available)
-Name of Composition
Medium (Instrumentation)
Record Company and Recording Number
Performer(s).

When several works by the same composer are included, the composer's name is omitted after the first entry. Similarly, when various recordings of the same composition are listed, the title of that particular work is omitted after the first mention.

The information is not cross-referenced by album title, since I have made an effort to list every composition individually. In other words, an album that includes music by different composers is listed by the particular composer's name, as opposed to the name of the album. It is my hope this system will prove quick and easy to use.

This discography deals entirely with music for which a written score i available. No improvisational music has been included, other than that which I considered to be of great pedagogical value. Jazz recordings such as those by vibraphonists Gary Burton, Milt Jackson, and Lionel Hampton or those featuring drumset artists have been omitted as it is almost impossible for one person to compile such a list. Similarly, traditional or ethnic music, such as that involving Indian, African, or Latin American drumming has also been excluded.

The title index at the end of the book is given as information to furthe facilitate the task of locating a particular work in the event that some of the information is missing (e.g., if the composer of a piece is not known, but the title of the work in question is available, you may look in this index, and find the page number where the composition is listed). The performer's index, in a similar fashion, is given so that you may locate a work should you know the performer's name, but not the composition tit or the composer of a particular work.

Furthermore, there is a list of addresses of all the different record companies involved in these recordings. This section is given to help the reader with the necessary information to obtain a particular recording were it not available in the market any longer.

This work represents my contribution to the percussion community after four and a half years of research. It is by no means the final word all available recordings for percussion, since new recordings emerge daily but I hope it will prove itself as a worthy beginning in terms of being a continuous source of reference for these great recordings. It is my intention to continue to update this information for the future as well, an would appreciate any comments or information that might benefit the ne edition. Any such information can be sent to me in care of the publisher.

I hope this book will be helpful to all who open it, and I wish you the best of listening in this delightful world of percussion literature.

Acknowledgements

For the past four years I have been compiling this information with the hope that I would someday publish it and with it make a significant contribution to the wide world of percussion research. As I see this project come to a reality, I would like to thank several people who at one time or another helped me with advice or information: Dr. Larry Vanlandingham, without whom this project would have never been started; Ms. Keiko Abe, for allowing me to search through her personal collection of records, and for her encouragement and continuous inspiration; Dr. Michael Udow, for invaluable advice through two years and for allowing me to use his collection of recordings; and the staff at Baylor University's Music Library, for the unsurmounted trust they placed in me by letting me browse freely through their wide collection of records.

None of this project would have been possible without the help of Truman and Virginia Netherton and to them go some very special thanks (we've been through a lot and I will always thank you for your care and ever-living love and patience!). On the same token, thank you DeWitts for all your help and encouragement through hard times with this book.

To my parents, family, and friends, thank you for all your support throughout the years!

I would also like to thank Marta Ptaszynska, Stuart Marrs, Atsuko Ibaraki, and Patricia Fisher, for contributing material for this edition; and Bismarck Fernández and Giancarlo Guerrero for their help with organizational matters. My thanks are also extended to the staff at the Computer Center of the University of Costa Rica for allowing me to use their equipment so extensively.

And to John Soroka, last in the list, but certainly not least, thank you always for all your priceless advice. You showed me the way to a much better state in our professional environment, and what a difference that made in my life! Thank you. This book is dedicated to all percussionists the world over, but to you in particular!

PERCUSSION DISCOGRAPHY

A

ABE, KEIKO (1940-   ) See also:
JAPANESE FOLK SONG

-Ancient Vase
For marimba.
Denon OF-7197-ND
KEIKO ABE (marimba).

Denon 33C0-1118 (Compact Disc)
KEIKO ABE (marimba).

-Dream of the Cherry Blossoms
For marimba.
Denon OF-7197-ND
KEIKO ABE (marimba).

Denon 33C0-1118 (Compact Disc)
KEIKO ABE (marimba).

-Frogs
For marimba.
Denon 33C0-1118 (Compact Disc)
KEIKO ABE (marimba).

-Little Windows
For marimba.
Denon 33C0-1118 (Compact Disc)
KEIKO ABE (marimba).

-Memories of the Seashore
For marimba.
Denon OF-7197-ND
KEIKO ABE (marimba).

Denon 33C0-1118 (Compact Disc)
KEIKO ABE (marimba).

-Mi-chi
For marimba.
Denon OF-7197-ND
KEIKO ABE (marimba).

Denon 33C0-1118 (Compact Disc)
KEIKO ABE (marimba).

-Prism
For marimba.
Denon OF-7197-ND
KEIKO ABE (marimba).

Denon 33C0-1118 (Compact Disc)
KEIKO ABE (marimba).

-She Died, My Water Lily Tonneke
(In cooperation with Walter Van
Hauwe)
Denon OF-7163-ND
KEIKO ABE (marimba) and WALTER
VAN HAUWE (recorder).

Denon 33C37-7393 (Compact Disc)
KEIKO ABE (marimba) and WALTER
VAN HAUWE (recorder).

-Torrent (In cooperation with
Walter Van Hauwe)
Denon OF-7163-ND
KEIKO ABE (marimba) and WALTER
VAN HAUWE (recorder).

Denon 33C37-7393 (Compact Disc)
KEIKO ABE (marimba) and WALTER
VAN HAUWE (recorder).

-Variations on Japanese Children's
Songs
For marimba.
Denon OF-7197-ND
KEIKO ABE (marimba).

Denon 33C0-1118 (Compact Disc)
KEIKO ABE (marimba).

-Wind in the Bamboo Grove
For marimba.
Denon OF-7197-ND
KEIKO ABE (marimba).

Denon 33C0-1118 (Compact Disc)
KEIKO ABE (marimba).

ABEJO, SISTER M. ROSALINA S.F.C.C
(1922-

-La Filipina "Imelda"
For marimba and orchestra.   (arr.
Sister M. Rosalina Abejo)
SRA 001
PETRA MOLAS (marimba). With the
PHILIPPINE SYMPHONY ORCHESTRA.
Sister M. Rosalina Abejo, conductor.

ABEL, ALAN

-Tom-Tom Foolery
For percussion quartet.
Torio PA-4010
KAZUKI MOMOSE, TOMOYUKI OKADA,
MITSUAKI IMAMURA, and SEIICHIRO
SADANARI (percussion).

ABIKO, YOSHIHIRO (1951-)

-Soh-oh (1979)
For clarinet, horn, piano, and two
percussionists.
Japan Federation of Composers JFC-
8012
ICHIRO HOSOYA and KEIZO KODAMI
(percussion).

ADAMS, JOHN LUTHER (1953-)

-Night Peace
Opus One 88
For soprano, harp, percussion and
chorus.

-Songbirdsongs
For piccolo, ocarina, and percussion.
Opus One 66

ADLER, SAMUEL (1928-)

-Four Dialogues
For euphonium and marimba.
Crystal   393
GORDON STOUT (marimba).

-Xenia. A Dialogue for Organ and
Percussion
Crystal   S-858
GORDON STOUT (percussion).

AGER KLAUS (1946-)

-I Remember a Bird (1976)
For clarinet, trombone, guitar,
piano, and percussion.
AUL (Aulos Schallplaten Viersen) 53
544

ALBRIGHT, WILLIAM (1944-)

-Take That (1972)
Opus One 22
BLACKEARTH PERCUSSION GROUP.

University of Michigan SM-0016
UNIVERSITY OF MICHIGAN
PERCUSSION ENSEMBLE. Charles
Owen, director.

ALEXANDER, JOSEF (1907-)

-Gitanjali (Song Offerings)
For soprano, harpsichord, and
percussion.
Orion   8244

-Three Diversions
For timpani and piano.
Serenus   12097

ALLAN, DOUGLAS R.

-Conflict
For percussion ensemble.
Golden Crest CR 4004

ALLDAHL, PER-GUNNAR (1943-)

-Stamma Blod
For male choir and drums.
BIS 32

ALLING, JOHN

-Afro-Fuga
For 4 high tom-toms, 4 chinese
temple blocks, bongo drums,
timbales, conga drums, and timpani.
Golden Crest CR-4016
ITHACA PERCUSSION ENSEMBLE.
Warren Benson, director.

ALLING, VERNON

-Overture de Ballet
For two percussionists.
Golden Crest CR-4016
ITHACA PERCUSSION ENSEMBLE.
Warren Benson, director.

ALRICH, ALEXIS (1955-)

-Palm Boulevard
For piano, mandolin, and marimba.
Opus One 104

AMEMIYA, YASUKAZU

-**Monochrome Sea** (1976)
For solo percussion and tape.
RCA JAPAN   RVC 2154
YASUKAZU AMEMIYA (percussion).

-**Summer Prayer ("Natsu Nebutsu")**
(1974)
For solo percussion, tape, and
percussion ensemble.
RCA JAPAN   RVC 2154
YASUKAZU AMEMIYA (solo
percussion).

ANDRIESSEN, JURRIAAN (1925-)

-**Summer Dances**

For guitar, harp, and percussion.
DAVS (DONEMUS AUDIO VISUAL
SERIES) 7273/3
NETHERLANDS PERCUSSION
ENSEMBLE.

ANDRIESSEN, LOUIS (1939-)

-**Hoketus**
For 2 pan-pipes, 2 Fender pianos, 2
pianos, 2 bass guitars, and 2 congas.
C.V.(COMPOSER'S VOICE) - DONEMUS
AUDIO VISUAL SERIES. 7702
PAUL KOEK AND HARRY GEURTS
(congas)

ANONYMOUS (18th C.)

-**Intraden in D. Nos. 1, 5, 11, and 14**
DGG ARC-73249
 CHRISTOPH CASKEL (percussion).

-**Piece for 8 obligato drums, 5 celli,**
and contrabass
SCHW VMS 2066
WERNER THÄRICHEN or NICHOLAS
BARDACH (kettledrums).

Schwann Musica Mundi CD 11066
(compact Disc)
WERNER THÄRICHEN or NICHOLAS
BARDACH (kettledrums).

ANTHEIL, GEORGE (1900-1959)

-**Ballet Mécanique**
Columbia Masterworks   ML 4956
THE NEW YORK PERCUSSION GROUP.
Carlos Surinach, conductor.

Teldec (Telefunken-Decca)   6.42196
AW
WILLY GOUDSWAARD and MICHAEL
DE ROO - XYLOPHONE; FRANS VAN DER
KRAAN - TIMPANI; ARTHUR CUNE,
HARRY GEURTS, LUC NAGTEGAAL,
and FRANC VAN DER STARRE
(percussion).

Urania   UR-134
LOS ANGELES CONTEMPORARY MUSIC
ENSEMBLE.   Robert Craft, conductor.

ARCURI, SERGE (1954-)

-**Chronaxie**
For percussion and tape.
Centredisques (Canada) WRC1-4951
BEVERLEY JOHNSTON (percussion).

ARETZ, ISABEL (1909-)

-**Movimientos de Percusión**
Ballet for 11 performers and 40
percussion instruments.
MTV LP-001

ARMA, PAUL (1905-)

-**In Memory of Béla Bartók**
For strings and percussion.
Hungaroton   12347

-**Two Resonances**
For percussion and piano.
Hungaroton SLPX 12615
ZOLTAN RACZ (percussion).

ARNDT, FELIX

-**Nola**
For xylophone solo and marimba
ensemble.
Mercury (Golden Imports)   SRI 75108
THE EASTMAN MARIMBA BAND.

Umbrella UMB DD-2
NEXUS.

ASHLEY, ROBERT (1930-   )

-Private Parts
For narrator, keyboards, and percussion.
Lovely LML 1001

-Untitled Mixes
For piano, bass, drums, and magnetic tape.
ESP-DISK 1009

B

BACH, JOHANN SEBASTIAN (1685-1750)

-Allegro (From **Concerto in A Minor for 4 Harpsichords and Orchestra. BWV 1065)**
CBS Records M-39704 Stereo
BRIAN SLAWSON (keyboard percussion).

CBS MK-39704 (Compact Disc)
BRIAN SLAWSON (keyboard percussion).

-Allegro (From **Concerto in C Major for 3 Harpsichords and Orchestra. BWV 1064)**
CBS Records M-39704 Stereo
BRIAN SLAWSON (keyboard percussion).

CBS MK-39704 (Compact Disc)
BRIAN SLAWSON (keyboard percussion).

-Allegro (From **Concerto in D Minor for Harpsichord and Orchestra. BWV 1052)**
CBS Records M-39704 Stereo
BRIAN SLAWSON (keyboard percussion).

CBS MK-39704 (Compact Disc)
BRIAN SLAWSON (keyboard percussion).

-"Christ lag in Todesbanden" (Chorale)
Musical Heritage Society MHS 7489 T Digital
LEIGH HOWARD STEVENS (marimba).

Musical Heritage Society MHC 9489 W (Cassette)
LEIGH HOWARD STEVENS (marimba).

Music Masters MMD 20124 K
LEIGH HOWARD STEVENS (marimba).

Music Masters MMD 60124 F (Compact Disc)
LEIGH HOWARD STEVENS (marimba).

-Fugue in C Major
Audio Fidelity 1812
NEW YORK PERCUSSION ENSEMBLE.

-Fugue in G minor
Croissant CRO-2001
REPERCUSSION.

Audio Fidelity 1812
NEW YORK PERCUSSION ENSEMBLE.

-Gavotte (From **French Suite No. 5)**
CBS Records M-39704 Stereo
BRIAN SLAWSON (keyboard percussion).

CBS MK-39704 (Compact Disc)
BRIAN SLAWSON (keyboard percussion).

-Gigue. (From **French Suite No. 5)**
CBS Records M-39704 Stereo
BRIAN SLAWSON (keyboard percussion).

CBS MK-39704 (Compact Disc)
BRIAN SLAWSON (keyboard percussion).

-Goldberg Variation No. 30
CBS Records M-39704 Stereo
BRIAN SLAWSON (keyboard percussion).

CBS MK-39704 (Compact Disc)
BRIAN SLAWSON (keyboard percussion).

-"Herzliebster Jesu" (Chorale)
Epic P-17808
VIDA CHENOWETH (marimba).

-"Herzliebster Jesu, was hast Du verbrochen" (Chorale)
Mallet Arts Inc. M-101
PAUL SMADBECK (marimba).

-**Invention VIII**
For marimba and vibraphone.
Thorofon MTH 149
PERCUSSION ENSEMBLE SIEGFRIED
FINK.

-**Jesu, Joy of Man's Desiring**
CBS Records M-39704 Stereo
BRIAN SLAWSON (keyboard
percussion).

CBS MK-39704 (Compact Disc)
BRIAN SLAWSON (keyboard
percussion).

-**Minuette in G**
CBS Records M-39704 Stereo
BRIAN SLAWSON (keyboard
percussion).

CBS MK-39704 (Compact Disc)
BRIAN SLAWSON (keyboard
percussion).

-**Musette in D Major**
CBS Records M-39704 Stereo
BRIAN SLAWSON (keyboard
percussion).

CBS MK-39704 (Compact Disc)
BRIAN SLAWSON (keyboard
percussion).

-**"Nun bitten wir den heiligen Geist"
(Chorale)**
Mallet Arts Inc.   M-101
PAUL SMADBECK (marimba).

-**Partita No. 3 in E Major, S. 1006.**
(arr.
T. Sasaki)
MHS 4856Y
TATSUO SASAKI (xylophone).

-**Prelude** (arr. Hartman) (from **Cello
Suite No.1**)
OMR 1001
ED HARTMAN (marimba).

-**Prelude and Fugue in Bb Major**
Musical Heritage Society MHS 7489 T
Digital
LEIGH HOWARD STEVENS (marimba).

Musical Heritage Society MHC 9489 W
(Cassette)
LEIGH HOWARD STEVENS (marimba).

Music Masters MMD 20124 K
LEIGH HOWARD STEVENS (marimba).

Music Masters MMD 60124 F (Compact
Disc)
LEIGH HOWARD STEVENS (marimba).

-**Prelude in G minor**
Musical Heritage Society MHS 7489 T
Digital
LEIGH HOWARD STEVENS (marimba).

Musical Heritage Society MHC 9489 W
(Cassette)
LEIGH HOWARD STEVENS (marimba).

Music Masters MMD 20124 K
LEIGH HOWARD STEVENS (marimba).

Music Masters MMD 60124 F (Compact
Disc)
LEIGH HOWARD STEVENS (marimba).

-**Sarabande** (arr. Hartman) (from
Cello Suite No.1)
OMR 1001
ED HARTMAN (marimba).

-**Sonata in A minor, S. 1001**
Musical Heritage Society MHS 7489 T
Digital
LEIGH HOWARD STEVENS (marimba).

Musical Heritage Society MHC 9489 W
(Cassette)
LEIGH HOWARD STEVENS (marimba).

Music Masters MMD 20124 K
LEIGH HOWARD STEVENS (marimba).

Music Masters MMD 60124 F (Compact
Disc)
LEIGH HOWARD STEVENS (marimba).

-**Sonata in B minor, S. 1003**
Musical Heritage Society MHS 7489 T
Digital
LEIGH HOWARD STEVENS (marimba).

Musical Heritage Society MHC 9489 W
(Cassette)
LEIGH HOWARD STEVENS (marimba).

Music Masters MMD 20124 K
LEIGH HOWARD STEVENS (marimba).

Music Masters MMD 60124 F (Compact Disc)
LEIGH HOWARD STEVENS (marimba).

-**Sonata in G minor**
Epic   P-17808
VIDA CHENOWETH (marimba).

-**Sonata No. 6 in E Major**
Studio 4 Productions   S4P R100
GORDON STOUT (marimba).

-**Toccata and Fugue in D minor**
Audio Fidelity 1812
NEW YORK PERCUSSION ENSEMBLE.

-**Toccata and Fugue in F Major**
Audio Fidelity 1812
NEW YORK PERCUSSION ENSEMBLE.

-**Two-Part Inventions:**
                    -**C Major.**
                    -**D minor.**
                    -**Bb Major.**
                    -**F Major.**
Musical Heritage Society MHS 7489 T
Digital
LEIGH HOWARD STEVENS (marimba).

Musical Heritage Society MHC 9489 W
(Cassette)
LEIGH HOWARD STEVENS (marimba).

Music Masters MMD 20124 K
LEIGH HOWARD STEVENS (marimba).

Music Masters MMD 60124 F (Compact Disc)
LEIGH HOWARD STEVENS (marimba).

BADINGS, HENK (1907-   )

-**Passacaglia for Tympany and Organ**
Lyrichord   7221

BAKER, DAVID (1931-   )

-**Concerto for 2 Pianos, Jazz Band, Strings, and Percussion**
Laurel   115

-**Singers of Songs/Weavers of Dreams**
For cello and 17 percussion instruments.
Golden Crest 4223 (D)
STEVEN BROWN (percussion).

Laurel   117
GEORGE GABER (percussion).

BARGIELSZKI, ZBIGNIEW (1937-   )

-**Ikar**
For alto sax, bass clarinet, vibraphone, and marimba.
IS (Intersound Munchen) PV 121
DUO CONTEMPORAIN.

-**Traumvogel**
For accordeon and percussion instruments.
IS (Intersound Munchen) PV 121
DUO CONTEMPORAIN.

BARRAQUE, JEAN (1928-1973)

-**Chant aprés Chant**
For 6 percussionists, voice, and piano.
AST (Astrée) AS 75
PERCUSSIONS COPENHAGUE. Brent Lyloff, director.

-**Sequence**
For percussion and diverse instruments.
AST (Astrée) AS 75
BRENT LYLOFF (percussion).

BARTLETT, HARRY

-**Four Holidays**
Urania   UX-106
AMERICAN PERCUSSION SOCIETY. Paul Price, conductor.

BARTOK, BELA (1881-1945)

-**Concerto for 2 Pianos, Percussion, and Orchestra (1940)**
Columbia   MS-6956
SAUL GOODMAN, WALTER ROSENBERGER, ELDEN BAILEY, and MORRIS LANG (percussion).

Hungaroton   11398
FERENC PETZ AND JOZSEF MARTON (percussion).

Philips 416 378-2 (Dig)

-Music for Strings, Percussion, and Celesta
Angel AM-34721 (Previously issued as ANG S-37512)
PHILADELPHIA ORCHESTRA. E. Ormandy, conductor.

Angel CDC-47117 (Compact Disc)
PHILADELPHIA ORCHESTRA. E. Ormandy, conductor.

Angel S-35949
BERLIN PHILHARMONIC. H. von Karajan, conductor.

Argo ZRG-657
ST. MARTIN'S ACADEMY. N. Marriner, conductor.

CBS MS-6956
NEW YORK PHILHARMONIC. L. Bernstein, conductor.

Columbia Masterworks MS-7206
BBC SYMPHONY. P. Boulez, conductor..

Denon CD-7122 (Compact Disc)
TOKYO METROPOLITAN SYMPHONY. Atzmon, conductor.

DG 2530 887
BOSTON SYMPHONY. S. Ozawa, conductor.

Hungaroton SLPX 1301
BUDAPEST SYMPHONY. G. Lehel, conductor.

London STS-15151
SUISSE ROMANDE. E. Ansermet, conductor.

RCA AGL 1-4087
CHICAGO SYMPHONY. F. Reiner, conductor.

Turnabout 34613
LONDON PHILHARMONIC. G. Solti, conductor.

Vox Cum Laude 9012
MINNESOTA SYMPHONY. Skrowaczewski, conductor.

-Romanian Folk Dances (arr. T. Sasaki)
MHS 4856Y
TATSUO SASAKI (xylophone).

-Sonata for 2 Pianos and Percussion
CBS Masterworks M 42625
DAVID CORKHILL and EVELYN GLENNIE (percussion)

Columbia Masterworks MS-6641
JEAN CLAUDE CASADESUS and JEAN PAUL DROUET (percussion).

DG 2530 964
CHRISTOPH CASKEL and HEINZ KONIG (percussion).

Hungaroton SLPX 11479
FERENC PETZ and JOZSEF MARTON (percussion).

London Argo 89
PARRY, LOVERIDGE, WEBSTER, and LEES QUARTET.

London CS-6583
TRISTAN FRY and JAMES HOLLAND (percussion).

Turnabout 4159
HARRY J. BAKER and EDWARD J. RUBSAN (percussion).

Turnabout TV-340365
OTTO SCHAD AND RICHARD SOHM (percussion).

Turnabout TV-S 34465
GUSTAV SCHUSTER, ROLAND BERGER, RUDOLPH MINARICH, and HEINRICH ZIMMERMANN (percussion).

BASHMAKOU, LEONID (1927-)

-Quattro Bagatelle
For flutes and percussion.
BIS 11
RAINER KUISMA (percussion).

BATES, ROBERT

-Five Movements
For bass and vibes.
Opus One 87
WILLIAM MOERSCH (vibes).

BAUER, JERZY (1936-)

-**Divertimento**
For two pianos and percussion.
MUZA SXL 0809

BRAUSZNERN, DIETRICH von (1928-)

-**Konzert**
For organ and percussion.
DC (Disco Center) Can 658 228
CHRISTOPH CASKEL (percussion).

BAZELON, IRWIN (1922-)

-**Sound Dreams**
For flute, clarinet, viola, cello, piano,
and percussion.
CRI S-486
FRANK EPSTEIN (percussion).

BECK, JOHN

-**Overture for Percussion**
King Records K-28C-165
MAKOTO ARUGA PERCUSSION
ENSEMBLE.

BECKER, FRANK

-**Stonehenge**
For flute, percussion, and
synthesizer.
Angel DS-37340 (D)

BECKER, JOHN J. (1886-1961)

-**The Abongo**
New World Records NW 285
THE NEW JERSEY PERCUSSION
ENSEMBLE. Raymond DesRoches,
conductor.

BEETHOVEN, LUDWIG VAN (1770-1827)

-**Scherzo from the 9th. Symphony**
(arr. Farberman)
MMG 115 (D)
THE ALL STAR PERCUSSION
ENSEMBLE. Harold Farberman,
conductor.

MMG MCD 10007 (Compact Disc)
THE ALL STAR PERCUSSION
ENSEMBLE. Harold Farberman,
conductor.

BEHREND, SIEGFRIED (1933-)

-**Mittelalterliche Tänze**
For guitar and percussion
instruments.
SCHW (Schwann-Bagel Dusseldorf)
HL 00 210

BENGUEREL, XAVIER (1931-)

-**Intento a Dos**
For guitar and percussion.
THO (Thorofon) MTH 218
SIEGFRIED FINK AND XAVIER JOAQUIN
(percussion).

-**Konzert (1976)**
For percussion and orchestra.
THO MTH 193
SIEGFRIED FINK (percussion).

-**Musica Per a Tres Percussionistes**
Caprice CAP 1280 (Sweden)
THE STOCKHOLM PERCUSSION
ENSEMBLE.

BENSON, WARREN (1924-)

-**Symphony for Drums and Wind Orchestra**
Cornell University 12
CORNELL PERCUSSION AND WIND
ENSEMBLE.

-**Three Pieces**
For percussion quartet.
Golden Crest CR-4016
ITHACA PERCUSSION ENSEMBLE.
Warren Benson, conductor.

-**Trio for Percussion (1957)**
For 3 tom-toms, 2 triangles, wood
block, suspended cymbal, maracas,
small gong,
and bass drum.
Orion 642
PRICE PERCUSSION ENSEMBLE.

Period Records SPL 743
PAUL PRICE, MICHAEL COLGRASS,
AND WARREN SMITH (percussion).

-**Variations on a Handmade Theme**
For eight hand-clappers.
Golden Crest CR-4016
THE ITHACA PERCUSSION ENSEMBLE.

BERGAMO, JOHN (1940-   )

-Almost Green
Creative Music Productions CMP-27-ST
JOHN BERGAMO (percussion).

CMP CD-27
JOHN BERGAMO (percussion).

-Beverly Hills (In cooperation with **Lucky Mosko** and **Larry Stein**)
Robey Records Rob. 1
REPERCUSSION UNIT

-5 X 5 X 5
Robey Records Rob. 1
REPERCUSSION UNIT

-Foreign Objects
Robey Records Rob. 1
REPERCUSSION UNIT

-Foreign Objects (Concert Recording)
Robey Records Rob. 1
REPERCUSSION UNIT

-Grand Ambulation of the Bb Zombies, The
CMP Records CMP 31 CS
REPERCUSSION UNIT

-Half the Distance to the Wall
CMP Records CMP 31 CS
REPERCUSSION UNIT

-I Feel More Like I Do Now Than I Did When I Got Here
Creative Music Productions CMP-27-ST
JOHN BERGAMO (percussion).

CMP CD-27
JOHN BERGAMO (percussion).

-Little Smegma, Son of Toecheese
Robey Records Rob. 1
REPERCUSSION UNIT

-Modelo
Creative Music Productions CMP-27-ST
JOHN BERGAMO (percussion).

CMP CD-27
JOHN BERGAMO (percussion).

-Nideggen Uthan
Creative Music Productions CMP-27-ST
JOHN BERGAMO (percussion).

CMP CD-27
JOHN BERGAMO (percussion).

-On The Edge
Creative Music Productions CMP-27-ST
JOHN BERGAMO (percussion).

CMP CD-27
JOHN BERGAMO (percussion).

-Piru Bole
Creative Music Productions CMP-27-ST
JOHN BERGAMO (percussion).

CMP CD-27
JOHN BERGAMO (percussion).

-The Sirene Of...
Creative Music Productions CMP-27-ST
JOHN BERGAMO (percussion).

CMP CD-27
JOHN BERGAMO (percussion).

-Square One
CMP Records CMP 31 CS
REPERCUSSION UNIT

-Whatever
Creative Music Productions CMP-27-ST
JOHN BERGAMO (percussion).

CMP CD-27
JOHN BERGAMO (percussion).

-Wuhan Darshan
Creative Music Productions CMP-27-ST
JOHN BERGAMO (percussion).

CMP CD-27
JOHN BERGAMO (percussion).

BERGER, GUNTHER (1929-   )

-Suite Francesa
For organ, clarinet, and timpani.
PSAL (Psallite) PET 37/050 567
JOSEPH SPULA (timpani).

BERGSMA, WILLIAM (1921-   )

-Changes for Seven (1971)
For piano and percussion.
(Originally for solo wind quintet,
harp, strings, and percussion).
Crystal S 258
MICHAEL CLARK (percussion).

BERIO, LUCIANO (1925-   )

-Circles
For female voice, harp, and two
percussionists.
Candide 31027

Mainstream 5005
Wergo Wer 60 021
JEAN-PIERRE DROUET and JEAN-
CLAUDE CASADESUS (percussion).

-Linea
For two pianos, vibraphone, and
marimba.
RCA Red Seal ARL 1-2291
JEAN-PIERRE DROUET (vibraphone)
and SYLVIO GUALDA (marimba).

BERLIOZ, HECTOR (1803-1869)

-March to the Scaffold (From
Symphonie Fantastique) (arr.
Farberman)
MMG 115 (D)
THE ALL STAR PERCUSSION
ENSEMBLE. Harold Farberman,
conductor.

MMG MCD 10007 (Compact Disc)
THE ALL STAR PERCUSSION
ENSEMBLE. Harold Farberman,
conductor.

BERTONCINI, MARIO (1932-   )

-Tune (1965)
For cymbals.
Opus One 22
BLACKEARTH PERCUSSION GROUP.

BEYER, FRANK MICHAEL (1928-   )

-Canti dei misteri. Nr. 2 (Cantus II)
For organ and percussion.
Chr (Christophorous Verlag
Freiburg) SCGLX 73 971
SIEGFRIED FINK (percussion).

BIZET, GEORGES (1838-1875)

-Carmen Fantasy (arr. Farberman)
MMG 115 (D)
THE ALL STAR PERCUSSION
ENSEMBLE.

MMG MCD 10007
THE ALL STAR PERCUSSION
ENSEMBLE.

BLAKEY ART (1919-   )

-Drum Suite
For percussion ensemble.
Columbia CL 1002

BLOMDAHL, KARL-BIRGER (1916-1968)

-Chamber Concerto
For winds, piano, and percussion.
M-G-M Records E-3371
THE M-G-M CHAMBER ORCHESTRA.
Carlos Surinach, conductor.

Swedish Society Discofil 33262

BLUME, JOACHIM (1923-   )

-Hymnus (1973)
For soprano and percussion.
CAM (Camerata) LPT 30 086
PAL KELO (percussion).

BOISSELET, PAUL

-Le Robot - Ballet Pantomime
Pour voix, piano, clavecin,
instruments électroniques, cordes,
batterie, et magnetophones.
SFP 30 006

-Symphonie Jaune (Symphony No. 2)
Pour timbale, batterie, petit
orchestra, clavecin, accordeon, et
instruments électroniques.
SFP 30 006

BOLCOM, WILLIAM (1938-   )

-**Black Host**
For organ, percussion, and tape.
Nonesuch 71260
SYDNEY HODKINSON (percussion).

-**Dream Music No. 2**
For percussion.
University of Michigan SM-0016
UNIVERSITY OF MICHIGAN
PERCUSSION ENSEMBLE. Charles
Owen, director.

BOND, VICTORIA (1945-   )

-**Peter Quince at the Clavier**
For Soprano, Piano, and Percussion.
Protone 150

BONIGHTON, IAN

-**Derivations III** (1972)
For percussion and tape.
Move MS-3016
THE AUSTRALIAN PERCUSSION
ENSEMBLE.

-**In Nomine** (1973)
For percussion, tape, and organ.
Move MS-3016
THE AUSTRALIAN PERCUSSION
ENSEMBLE.

-**One, Two, Three** (1974)
For three percussionists.
Move MS-3016
THE AUSTRALIAN PERCUSSION
ENSEMBLE.

BONS, JOEL (1952-   )

-**Sextet**
For violin, clarinet, mandolin, guitar,
marimba, and double bass.
Composers' Voice   CV 8204

BOONE, CHARLES (1939-   )

-**Shunt**
For three   drummers.
Grenadilla 1063

BØRUP-JØRGENSEN, AXEL (1924-   )

-**Music for Percussion and Viola. Op. 18**
Paula 15 (Denmark)

-**Schlussstück. Op. 50**
For 16 voices, piano, harpsichord,
and percussion.
Paula 15 (Denmark).

BOUCOURECHLIEV, ANDRÉ (1925-   )

-**Archipel I**
For two pianos, and 54 percussion
instruments.
Angel S-36655
JEAN-CLAUDE CASADESUS and JEAN-
PIERRE DROUET (percussion).

-**Ulysse** (1981)
For flute and percussion.
CDM LDX 78.700
JEAN-PIERRE DROUET (percussion).

BOULEZ, PIERRE (1925-   )

-**Le Marteau sans maître** (1955)
For alto, viola, flute, xylorimba,
vibraphone, guitar, and percussion.
Ades 14008 PSI

Harmonia Mundi 1C065   99831
GEORGES van GUCHT (xylorimba),
CLAUDE RICOU (vibraphone),   and
JEAN BATIGNE (percussion).

Turnabout   34081
GEORGES van GUCHT (xylorimba),
CLAUDE RICOU (vibraphone),   and
JEAN BATIGNE (percussion).

CBS 76.191

BRANT, HENRY (1913-   )

-**Galaxy 2**
For piccolo, clarinet, 2 solo horns,
trumpet, trombone, glockenspiel, and
6 timpani.
Columbia Masterworks ML 4956
ALFRED HOWARD (timpani) and
MORRIS GOLDENBERG (glockenspiel).

-Machinations
For winds, harp, percussion, and organ.
Desto 7108

-Signs and Alarms
For piccolo, 2 clarinets, 2 horns, solo trumpet, solo trombone, tuba, marimba, xylophone, and 4 timpani.
Columbia Masterworks ML 4956
ALFRED HOWARD (timpani) and MORRIS GOLDENBERG (marimba and xylophone).

BREHM, ALVIN (1925-   )

-Dialogues (1936)
For bassoon and percussion.
Golden Crest 7019
PAUL PRICE (percussion).

BRETTINGHAM SMITH, JULYON (1949-   )

-Two Old Songs (1979)
For baritone, guitar, and percussion.
IS PV 104
KLAUS KIESSNER (percussion).

BREUER, HARRY (1901-   )

-Back Talk
For xylophone solo and marimba accompaniment.
Mercury (Golden Imports) SRI 75108
THE EASTMAN MARIMBA BAND.

Second Hearing GS 9008 (Compact Disc)
UNIVERSITY OF OKLAHOMA PERCUSSION ENSEMBLE.

-Back Talk (arr. **Floyd Werle**)
Record not for sale
RANDALL EYLES (marimba) With the USAF BAND.

-Bit O'Rhythm
For xylophone solo and marimba accompaniment.
Mercury (Golden Imports) SRI 75108
THE EASTMAN MARIMBA BAND.

-Four Stick Joe
Croissant CRO-2001
REPERCUSSION.

Second Hearing GS 9008 (Compact Disc)
UNIVERSITY OF OKLAHOMA PERCUSSION ENSEMBLE.

-Joplin on Wood
Lang Percussion Company - New York (Cassette only)
HARRY BREUER (xylophone).

-Mallets A La Zurke
Lang Percussion Company - New York (Cassette only)
HARRY BREUER (xylophone).

-On the Woodpile
For xylophone solo and marimba accompaniment.
Mercury (Golden Imports) SRI 75108
THE EASTMAN MARIMBA BAND.

-Powder Puff
For xylophone solo and marimba accompaniment.
Mercury (Golden Imports) SRI 75108
THE EASTMAN MARIMBA BAND.

-Rag Doll Rag
Lang Percussion Company - New York (Cassette only)
HARRY BREUER (xylophone).

-Temptation Revamp
Lang Percussion Company - New York (Cassette only)
HARRY BREUER (xylophone).

-Waltz in Ragtime
Lang Percussion Company - New York (Cassette only)
HARRY BREUER (xylophone).

BROWER, LEO (1939-   )

-Variantes
For one percussionist.
Wergo WER 60123
ELMAR KOLB (percussion).

Wergo 60123-50 (Compact Disc)
ELMAR KOLB (percussion).

BROWN, EARLE (1926-   )

-Four Systems
For 4 amplified cymbals.
Columbia MS-7139
MAX NEUHAUS (cymbals)

BROWN, RAYNER

-Concerto
For two pianos, brass, and percussion.
WIM 8
ERIC REMSEN (percussion).

-Five Pieces.
For organ, harp, brass, and
percussion.
Avant 1001

BRÜN, HERBERT (1918-   )

-Hit or Miss? (1968/75)
Non Sequitur Records 1 to 3
ALLEN OTTE and GARY KVISTAD
(percussion).

-More Dust. (1977)
Opus One 80/81
THE PERCUSSION GROUP -
CINCINNATI.

-Musik beispiele fuer das buch: eber musik und zum computer
Orphi 1 OPAL 60.205
ALLAN O'CONNOR and WILLIAM
YOUHASS (percussion).

-Non Sequitur VI (1966)
For flute, cello, harp, piano, and
percussion.
Non Sequitur Records 1 to 3
ALLAN O'CONNOR and WILLIAM
YOUHASS (percussion).

-Non Sequitur VI (Fragment)
For flute, cello, harp, piano, and
percussion.
Orphi 1 OPAL 60.205
ALLAN O'CONNOR and WILLIAM
YOUHASS (percussion).

-Nonet (1969)
For flute, violin, clarinet, trumpet,
french horn, trombone, bassoon,
double bass, and percussion.
Non Sequitur Records 1 to 3
MICHAEL UDOW (percussion).

-Plot
Orphi 1 OPAL 60.205
MICHAEL RANTA (percussion).

-Sonoriferous Loops
For flute, trumpet, double bass, and
percussion.
Non Sequitur Records 1 to 3
WILLIAM PARSONS, MICHAEL ROSEN,
and JOHN DUTTON (percussion).

-Sonoriferous Loops (Fragment)
For flute, trumpet, double bass, and
percussion.
Orphi 1 OPAL 60.205
WILLIAM PARSONS, MICHAEL ROSEN,
and JOHN DUTTON (percussion).

-Stalks and Trees and Drops and Clouds
Orphi 1 OPAL 60.205
WILLIAM YOUHASS (percussion).

-Touch and Go
Orphi 1 OPAL 60.205
ALLAN O'CONNOR (percussion).

-Trio for Flute. Double Bass, and Percussion
Non Sequitur Records 1 to 3
MICHAEL UDOW (percussion).

-Trio for Trumpet, Trombone, and Percussion (1966)
Non Sequitur Records 1 to 3
JAMES HARRIS (percussion).

BUBALO, RUDOLPH (1927-   )

-Five Pieces
For brass quintet and percussion.
Advent Records USR 5004
JOSEPH ADATO and THOMAS ROBERTS
(percussion).

Crystal S-533
DONALD MILLER and ROBERT MATSON
(percussion).

BUCZYNSKI, PAWEL

-Nokturn/Nocturne
MUZA SX 2092
WARSAW PERCUSSION GROUP.

BUGGERT, ROBERT (1918-)

-Introduction and Fugue
For marimba, piano, snare drum, small tom-tom, bongo drums, large tom-toms, xylophone, wood block, maracas, tenor drum, triangle, suspended cymbal, timpani, chimes, bass drum, and gong.
Golden Crest CR-4016
THE ITHACA PERCUSSION ENSEMBLE. Warren Benson, director.

BUSSOTTI, SYLVANO (1931-)

-Coeur pour batteur - Positively Yes
Columbia MS-7139
MAX NEUHAUS (percussion).

-Rara Requiem
For voice, guitar, cello, wind instruments, piano, harp, and percussion.
DG 2530 754
ZAMBRANO (percussion).

C

CAGE, JOHN (1912-)

-Amores (1943)
For prepared piano, 3 high, 3 medium, and 3 low tom-toms, and 3 high, 2 medium, and 2 low wood blocks.
BIS 272 (D)
KROUMATA PERCUSSION ENSEMBLE.

BIS CD 272 (Compact Disc)
KROUMATA PERCUSSION ENSEMBLE.

Mainstream Records M/S 5011
JOHN CAGE (prepared piano); PAUL PRICE, RAYMOND DesROCHES, and GEORGE BOBERG (percussion)

Opus One 22
BLACKEARTH PERCUSSION GROUP.

-Double Music (1941) (In cooperation with LOU HARRISON)
For 6 water-buffalo bells, 11 brake drums, 2 sistrums, 6 sleighbells, thundersheet, 3 japanese temple gongs, 2 large tam-tams, 6 cowbells, 6 muted gongs, and water gong.

Cal CAL 30 492
WURZBURG MUSIC SCHOOL PERCUSSION ENSEMBLE. Siegfried Fink, conductor.

Mainstream Records M/S 5011
PAUL PRICE, GEORGE BOBERG, RAYMOND DesROCHES, and EDWARD CORNELIUS (percussion).

New World Records NW 330
THE NEW MUSIC CONSORT.

Time 58000
MANHATTAN PERCUSSION ENSEMBLE. Paul Price, conductor.

-First Construction in Metal
D-MMG 105
LONDON PERCUSSION ENSEMBLE.

Philips Stereo 6718 040
LES PERCUSSIONS DE STRASBOURG.

Philips 32 CD 3063 (Compact Disc)
LES PERCUSSIONS DE STRASBOURG.

-Fontana Mix - Feed for 4-12 Adjustable Resistances
Mass Art M-133
MAX NEUHAUS (percussion).

-Second Construction (1940)
For percussion quartet.
BIS 232 (D)
KROUMATA PERCUSSION ENSEMBLE.

BIS CD-232 (Compact Disc)
KROUMATA PERCUSSION ENSEMBLE.

Hungaroton HCD 12855 (Compact Disc)
AMADINDA PERCUSSION GROUP.

Hungaroton SLPD 12800
AMADINDA PERCUSSION GROUP.

New World Records NW 330
THE NEW MUSIC CONSORT.

-She is Asleep
For twelve tom-toms.
Thorofon CTH 2003 (Compact Disc)
WURZBURGER PERKUSSIONS ENSEMBLE. Siegfried Fink, director.

THO MTH 149
PERCUSSION ENSEMBLE SIEGFRIED
FINK.

-**Third Construction** (1941)
For percussion quartet.
New World Records 319
THE NEW MUSIC CONSORT.

Nexus NE 05
NEXUS.

-**27'10.554"**
For a percussionist.
Finnadar 9017
DONALD KNAACK (percussion).

-**Variations III**
For voices and percussion.
DGG 139 442
GERD ZACHER and ALLENDE BLIN
(percussion).

Wergo Wer 60 057
THE SAN FRANCISCO CONSERVATORY
NEW MUSIC ENSEMBLE.

CAHN, WILLIAM

-**Birds, The**
Nexus NE 01
NEXUS.

-**Changes** (1981)
Nexus NE 05
NEXUS.

CAMPO, FRANK

-**Commedie**
For trombone and percussion.
Avant 1006
MITCHELL PETERS (percussion).

-**Dualidad**
For bass clarinet and percussion.
WIM 10
MITCHELL PETERS (percussion).

CARNO, ZITA

-**Sextet**
For percussion.
IRC APD 075 S
THE FREDONIA PERCUSSION
ENSEMBLE. Theodore Frazeur,
director.

University of Michigan SM-0016
UNIVERSITY OF MICHIGAN
PERCUSSION ENSEMBLE. Charles
Owen, director.

CARTER, ELLIOT (1908-   )

-**Eight Pieces for Four Timpani**
BIS 256
GERT MORTENSEN (timpani).

Odyssey Y-34137
MORRIS LANG (timpani).

-**Pieces for timpani (1949-1966)
(Recitative, Moto Perpetuo, Saeta,
Improvisation).**
Erato R32E-1019 (Compact Disc)
SYLVIO GUALDA (timpani).

Erato STU-71106
SYLVIO GUALDA (timpani).

CHADABE, JOEL (1938-   )

-**Rhythms**
For percussion and tape.
Lovely VR-1301

CHAITKIN, DAVID (1938-   )

-**Serenade**
For flute, piano, violin, cello, double
bass, vibraphone, glockenspiel, and
tubular bells.
CRI SD-493
DANIEL DRUCKMAN (vibraphone
and glockenspiel); JAMES BAKER
(tubular bells).

CHANCE, NANCY LAIRD (1931-   )

-**Daysongs**
For flute and percussion.
Opus One 72
GLEN VELEZ and JAMES PREISS
(percussion).

-**Exultation and Lament**
For alto sax and timpani.
Opus One 79
WILLIAM TRIGG (timpani).

-Ritual Sounds (1975)
For brass and percussion.
Opus One 69
J. KRAUS, G. SCHALL, and G. VELEZ
(percussion).

CHARPENTIER, JACQUES

-Lolita
For ondes martenot and percussion.
MHS 821
DIDIER DUCLOS (percussion).

CHATMAN, STEPHEN

-Quiet Exchange
For clarinet and suspended cymbals.
Opus One 46
KENNETH MOORE (cymbals).

CHAVEZ, CARLOS (1899-1978)

-Toccata for Percussion
Boston Records B-207
BOSTON PERCUSSION GROUP.

Columbia Masterworks ML 5847
THE LOS ANGELES PERCUSSION
ENSEMBLE. William Kraft, director.

CSP AMS-6447
THE LOS ANGELES PERCUSSION
ENSEMBLE.

King Records K-28C-165
MAKOTO ARUGA PERCUSSION
ENSEMBLE.

Philips Stereo 6718 040
LES PERCUSSIONS DE STRASBOURG.

Philips 32 CD 3063 (Compact Disc)
LES PERCUSSIONS DE STRASBOURG.

Urania UR 134
THE MANHATTAN PERCUSSION
ENSEMBLE. Paul Price, conductor.

Urania URLP 7144
ELDEN BAILEY, CARROLL C.
BRATMAN, GEORGE GABER, MORRIS
LANG, ARTHUR LAYFIELD, and
WALTER ROSENBERGER (percussion).

-Hochipilli Macuilxochitl
For mexican orchestra.
Col LS-1016

CHIHARA, PAUL (1938-   )

-Beauty of the Rose is in its Passing
For bassoon, two horns, harp, and
percussion.
Crystal S-352

-Branches
For two bassoons and percussion.
CRI SD 269
KENNETH WATSON (percussion).

-Ceremony I
For oboe, celli, double bass, and
percussion.
Turnabout QTV-S 34572
MICHAEL FRYE (percussion).

-Ceremony II (Incantations)
For flute, two cellos, and percussion.
New World Records 237

-Redwood
For viola and percussion.
Protone 145
KENNETH WATSON (percussion).

-Willow Willow
For bass flute, tuba, trombones, and
percussion.
CRI SD 269
KAREN ERVIN, KENNETH WATSON,
and PAUL CHIHARA (percussion).

CHOPIN, FREDERICK (1810-1849)

-Polonaise Militaire, (arr. G. H. Green.)
Conservatory 7101 M
GEORGE HAMILTON GREEN
(xylophone).

CHRISTIAN, BOBBY

-Poem for Percussion
Torio PA-4010
MITSUAKI IMAMURA, TADASHI
SETOGAWA, YOSHITAKA KOBAYASHI,
KAZUKI MOMOSE, TOMOYUKI OKADA,
and SEIICHIRO SADANARI
(percussion).

CIRONE, ANTHONY (1941-)

-Double Concerto
For piano and percussion.
Crystal 140
SONIC BOOM PERCUSSION ENSEMBLE.

-4/4 for Four
Sonic LS-11 (Dir)
SONIC ARTS PERCUSSION ENSEMBLE.

-Japanese Impressions
Sonic LS-11 (Dir)
SONIC ARTS PERCUSSION ENSEMBLE.

-Overture
Sonic LS-11 (Dir)
SONIC ARTS PERCUSSION ENSEMBLE.

-Triptych
Crystal 140
SONIC BOOM PERCUSSION ENSEMBLE.

Sonic LS-11 (Dir)
SONIC ARTS PERCUSSION ENSEMBLE.

COLGRASS, MICHAEL (1932-)

**-Chamber Music for Percussion
Quintet**
(1954)
CRS 6 (U of I School of Music Custom
Recording Series)
UNIVERSITY OF ILLINOIS
PERCUSSION ENSEMBLE - Jack
McKenzie, conductor.

-Déjà Vu (1977)
For percussion quartet and
orchestra.
New World Records NW 318
RICHARD HOLMES, JOHN KASICA,
RICH O'DONNELL, and THOMAS
STUBBS (percussion).

-Fantasy Variations (1961)
For 8 chromatic drums and
percussion sextet.
IRC APD 075 S
NEIL DePONTE (8 chromatic drums)
and THE FREDONIA PERCUSSION
ENSEMBLE. Theodore Frazeur,
conductor.

Nonesuch H-71291
JOSEPH PASSARO (8 chromatic
drums) and THE NEW JERSEY
PERCUSSION ENSEMBLE. Raymond
DesRoches, conductor.

Elektra/Nonesuch 9 79150-2
(Compact Disc)
JOSEPH PASSARO (8 chromatic
drums) and THE NEW JERSEY
PERCUSSION ENSEMBLE. Raymond
DesRoches, conductor.

-Light Spirit (1963)
For flute, viola, guitar,and
percussion.
New World Records NW 318
RICH O'DONNELL (percussion).

-Percussion Music
For 4 temple blocks, 4 toy drums, 4
high tom-toms, and 4 deep tom-toms.
Orion 7276
MANHATTAN PERCUSSION ENSEMBLE.
Paul Price, conductor.

Orion 642
Period Records SPL 743
PAUL PRICE, MICHAEL COLGRASS,
PHILIP BROWN, and WARREN SMITH
(percussion).

-Three Brothers
Golden Crest CR 4004

Urania UX-106
AMERICAN PERCUSSION SOCIETY

-Variations for Four Drums and Viola
Crystal S-133
FRANK EPSTEIN (four drums).
RCA Victor LSC 6184
VIC FIRTH (four drums).

CONSTANT, MARIUS (1926-)

-Psyche
For 2 pianos and percussion.
Erato STU 71-238
SYLVIO GUALDA and JEAN-PIERRE
DROUET (percussion).

-Quatorze Stations
For percussion and six instruments.
Erato R32E-1018 (Compact Disc)
SYLVIO GUALDA (percussion).

Erato STU 70-603
SYLVIO GUALDA (percussion).

COPE, DAVID (1941-   )

-Margins
For trumpet, cello, percussion, and
two pianos.
Orion 75169

CORELLI, ARCANGELO (1653-1713)

-Christmas Concerto (From Concerto Grosso, Op. 6, No. 8)
CBS Records M39704 Stereo
BRIAN SLAWSON (keyboard
percussion).

COULOMBE SAINT-MARCOUX, MICHELINE (1938-   )

-Trakadie
For solo percussion.
CBC RCI/CAPAC RM-222
GUY LACHAPELLE (percussion).

COWELL, HENRY (1897-1965)

-Ostinato Pianissimo (1934)
For string piano, 8 rice bowls,
marimba, xylophone, tambourine, 2
wood blocks, guiro, bongo drums, 3
drums, and 3 gongs.
Mainstream Records MS/5011
ZITA CARNO, CHARLES BURKHART,
RAY DesROCHES, GEORGE BOBERG,
EDWARD CORNELIUS, DAMON
BUCKLEY, RICHARD ALLEN, and
GERALD JACOBOSKY (percussion).

Nonesuch H-71291
NEW JERSEY PERCUSSION ENSEMBLE.
Raymond DesRoches, conductor.

Elektra/Nonesuch 9 79150-2
(Compact Disc)
NEW JERSEY PERCUSSION ENSEMBLE.
Raymond DesRoches, conductor.

Thorofon CTH 2003 (Compact Disc)
WURZBURGER PERKUSSIONS
ENSEMBLE.   Siegfried Fink, director.

Tho MTH 149
PERCUSSION ENSEMBLE SIEGFRIED
FINK.

Time 58000
MANHATTAN PERCUSSION ENSEMBLE.
Paul Price, conductor.

-Pulse (1939)
For percussion sextet.
BIS 232 (D)
KROUMATA PERCUSSION ENSEMBLE.

BIS CD-232 (Compact Disc)
KROUMATA PERCUSSION ENSEMBLE.

New World 319
NEW MUSIC CONSORT.

-Set of Five
For violin, piano, and percussion.
M-G-M Records E-3454
ELDEN BAILEY - PERCUSSION.

CRESTON, PAUL (1906- 1985)

-Concertino for Marimba, Op. 21
Aul 53 576
WOLFGANG PACHLA (marimba).
With the Nurnmberg Symphony
Orchestra.   Erich Kloss, cond. -
Complete Version (Mvts. 1, 2, and 3).

CBS MS-6977
CHARLES OWEN (marimba). With the
Philadelphia Orchestra.   Eugene
Ormandy, cond.   First movement
only.

Classic Performances #1 CMP-VC1
(Cassette)
VIDA CHENOWETH (marimba). With
the Orchestra of America.   Richard
Korn, cond. Complete version (Mvts.
1, 2, and 3).

Studio 4 Productions S4P-R102
GORDON STOUT (marimba). With
piano accompaniment.   Complete
version (Mvts. 1, 2, and 3).

CRUMB, GEORGE (1929-   )

-Ancient Voices of Children (1970)
For mezzo-soprano, boy soprano,
oboe, mandolin, harp, electric piano,
and percussion.
Nonesuch H-71255
RAYMOND DesROCHES, RICHARD FITZ,
and HOWARD VAN HYNING
(percussion).

Nonesuch 79149-2 (Compact Disc)
RAYMOND DesROCHES, RICHARD FITZ,
and HOWARD VAN HYNING
(percussion).

-**Madrigals (Books I-IV)** (1965-69)
For soprano and instrumental
ensemble.
BIS LP-261/62 (D)
SEPPO ASIKAINEN (percussion).

BIS CD-261 (Compact Disc)
SEPPO ASIKAINEN - PERCUSSION.

-**Makrokosmos III (Music for a
Summer Evening)** (1974)
For 2 amplified pianos and
percussion.
AMU ETST-038
WOLFGANG LINDNER and KARL
PEINKOFER (percussion).

BIS LP-261/62 (D)
RAINER KUISMA and SEPPO
ASIKAINEN (percussion).

BIS CD-261 (Compact Disc)
RAINER KUISMA and SEPPO
ASIKAINEN (percussion).

Nonesuch 71311
RAYMOND DesROCHES and RICHARD
FITZ (percussion).

Nonesuch 79149-2 (Compact Disc)
RAYMOND DesROCHES, RICHARD FITZ
(percussion).

-**Night Music I**
For soprano, celesta, piano, and
percussion.
Candide 31113

CRI-S-218

CRI-ACS-6008

-**Night of the Four Moons** (1969)
CBS M-32739
AEOLIAN CHAMBER PLAYERS.

CUMMINGS, CONRAD (1948-)

-**Summer Air**
For flute, oboe, soprano sax, violin,
viola, cello, harp, and percussion.
CRI SD-487
CLAIRE HELDRICH and WILLIAM A.
TRIGG (percussion).

D

DRETWYLER, JEAN (1907-)

-**Capriccio, Andante et Humoresque**
For piccolo, alphorn, percussion,
and strings.
Gallo 30-239
ALAIN RAMIREZ (percussion).

-**Concerto**
For trumpet, strings, and percussion.
Gallo 30-172

-**Trois Danses**
For percussion and strings.
Gallo 30-239
ALAIN RAMIREZ (percussion).

DAHL, INGOLF (1912-1970)

-**Duettino Concertante**
For flute and percussion.
Crystal 641
KAREN ERVIN (percussion).

Grenadilla 1042
THEODORE FRAZEUR (percussion).

-**Variations on a Swedish Folk Tune**
(arr. Frazeur)
For flute and percussion.
CRS 8425

DAO, NGUYEN-THIEN (1940-)

-**May**
For solo percussion.
Erato R32E-1019 (Compact Disc)
SYLVIO GUALDA (percussion).

Erato STU-71106
SYLVIO GUALDA (percussion).

DAVIDOVSKY, MARIO (1934-   )

- Synchronisms No. 5
For percussion ensemble and
electronic   sounds.
CRI SD-268
RAYMOND DesROCHES, RICHARD FITZ,
CLAIRE HELDRICH, DONALD
MARCONE, and HOWARD VAN HYNING
(percussion).

Turnabout TV-S 34487
THE GROUP FOR CONTEMPORARY
MUSIC.

DEASON, DAVID (1945-   )

-Chamber Concerto (1981)
For horn and percussion.
Crystal S-673
INDIANA PERCUSSION ENSEMBLE.
George Gaber, director.

DECSENYI, JANOS (1927-   )

-Sándor Weores' Twelfth Symphony
(1980)
For soprano and percussion
Hungaroton SLPX 12556
RACZ and VACZI (percussion).

DeFOTIS, WILLIAM

-Continuous Showing (1978)
Opus One 80/81
THE PERCUSSION GROUP -
CINCINNATI.

DeFRIES-D'ALBERT, BEVERLY (1944-   )

-Mental Sailing
For electric strings, piano, and
timpani.
Coronet 3110

-Nosce Teipsum
For voice, zither, and percussion.
Coronet 3110

DePONTE, NEIL

-Concertino for Marimba
Studio 4 Productions S4P-R102
GORDON STOUT (marimba).

-Forest Rain
Instructional Resources Center APD
075 S
THE FREDONIA PERCUSSION
ENSEMBLE.

DIONNE, VINCENT

-Chaka
Croissant CRO-2001
REPERCUSSION.

-Château du Carte
Croisant CRO-2001
REPERCUSSION.

DLUGOSZEWSKI, LUCIA (1931-   )

-Tender Theatre Flight Nagerie
For brass and percussion.
CRI S-388

DOI, YOSHIYUKI

-Monolog for Marimba
CBS Sony 32 DC 5027 (Compact Disc)
MICHIKO TAKAHASHI (marimba).

DONOVAN, RICHARD FRANK (1891-
1970)

-Soundings
For bassoon, trumpet, and
percussion.
M-G-M Records E-3371
THE M-G-M CHAMBER ENSEMBLE.
Carlos Surinach, conductor.

DOWLAND, JOHN

-Pavana Lachrimae Antique
Denon OF-7163-ND
KEIKO ABE (marimba) and WALTER
VAN HAUWE (recorder).

Denon 33C37-7393 (Compact Disc)
KEIKO ABE (marimba) and WALTER
VAN HAUWE (recorder).

DOYLE, ROGER

-Oizzo No
For electronic sounds and
instrumental ensemble.
Thrust Records 3
ROGER DOYLE (drums).

DRUCKMAN, JACOB (1928-)

-**Animus II**
For percussion, voice, and tape.
CRI S-255
RICHARD FITZ and GORDON GOTTLIEB
(percussion).

DUBROVAY, LASZLO

-**Six Duets**
For violin and percussion.
Hungaroton SLPX 12065
GABOR KOSA (percussion).

DUCHAMP, MARCEL (1887-1968)

-**The Bride Stripped Bare By Her Bachelors, Even**
Finlandia 9017
DONALD KNAACK (percussion).

DUCKWORTH, WILLIAM E. (1943-)

-**Gambit**
For percussion and tape.
Capra 1210
WILLIAM YOUHASS (percussion).

E

EISMA, WILL (1929-)

-**Le gibet**
For baritone, oboe, flute, clarinet,
violin, piano, cello, and percussion.
Composers' Voice (DAVS) 7475/2

ELMENREICH, (?)

-**The Spinning Song**
CBS Records M-39704 Stereo
BRIAN SLAWSON (keyboard
percussion).

CBS MK-39704 (Compact Disc)
BRIAN SLAWSON (keyboard
percussion).

ENGELMAN, JOHN

-**Fanfare**
For marimba, xylophone, triangle,
suspended cymbal, snare drum, tom-
tom, large gong, bass drum, small
gong, and 4 timpani.
GC CR-4016
ITHACA PERCUSSION ENSEMBLE.
Warren Benson, director.

ENGLUND, SVEN EINAR (1916-)

-**Symphony No. 4**
For strings and percussion.
Finlandia 329 PSI

ERB, DONALD (1927-)

-**Concerto for Solo Percussionist**
Turnabout 34433
MARVIN DAHLGREEN (percussion).

-**Devil's Quickstep, The** (1938)
For winds, piano, strings, and
percussion.
Spectrum SR-195

-**Diversion for Two (Other than Sex)**
(1966)
For trumpet and percussion.
Opus One S-1
TELE LESBINES (percussion).

-**Harold's Trip to the Sky** (1972)
For viola, piano, and percussion.
Crystal 531

-**Reconossaince**
For violin, double bass, piano,
percussion, Moog synthesizer, and
Moog polyphonic instrument.
Nonesuch H-71 223

-**Spatial Fanfare**
For brass and percussion.
Louisville 772

-**Trio** (1977)
For violin, keyboards, and
percussion.
Crystal S-505

ERDMAN, DIETRICH (1917-   )

-Duo
For clarinet and percussion.
MRS (Marus) 30 8119 Z
JOACHIM WINKLER (percussion).

-Episodes (1970)
For guitar and percussion.
THO MTH 169
WOLFGANG SCHNEIDER (percussion).

-Musica per Quattro
For 3 woodwinds and percussion.
MRS (Marus) 30 8119 Z
JOACHIM WINKLER (percussion).

-Notturni
For clarinet and percussion.
MRS (Marus) 30 8119 Z
JOACHIM WINKLER (percussion).

EUTENEUER-ROHRER, URSULA HENRIETTA
(1953-   )

-Schlagzeugquartett
SST (Sound Star - Tonprod.) 0 164
SCHLAGZEUGENSBL. d. BADISCHEN
KONSERVAT.

-Trios No. 4 and No. 5
For accordeon, piano, and
percussion instruments.
SST (Sound Star - Tonprod.) 0 164
SCHLAGZEUGENSBL. d. BADISCHEN
KONSERVAT.

F

FARBERMAN, HAROLD (1929-   )

-Alea
For six percussionists.
Serenus 12064
PUGWASH PERCUSSION ENSEMBLE.

-Evolution. Music for Percussion,
French Horn, and Soprano
Boston Records B-207
BOSTON PERCUSSION GROUP.

MMG 105 (D)
LONDON PERCUSSION ENSEMBLE.

FELCIANO, RICHARD (1930-   )

-The Angels of Turtle Island
For soprano, flute, violin,
percussion, and tape.
Grenadilla 1063

-Glossolalia
For baritone, percussion, organ, and
electronics.
Cambridge 2560
PETER MAUND (percussion).

FELDMAN, MORTON (1926-   )

-Chorus and Instruments II
Odyssey 32160155
JOHN BERGAMO (chimes).

-For Frank O'Hara
For flute, clarinet, violin, cello,
piano, and percussion.
Odyssey Y-34138

-The King of Denmark
Columbia MS-7139
MAX NEUHAUS (percussion).

RCA Japan RVC 2154
AMEMIYA YASUKAZU (percussion).

-Rothko Chapel
For chorus, viola, and percussion.
Odyssey Y-34138
JAMES HOLLAND (percussion).

FINK, SIEGFRIED (1928-   )

-Bagatella
For 2 pianos and percussion.
THO MTH 218
SIEGFRIED FINK and XAVIER JOAQUIN
(percussion).

-Bearb: Duo Concertante
For vibraphone and guitar.
AUD 63 403
BERND KREMLING (vibraphone).

-Beat the Beat
Thorofon CTH 2003 (Compact Disc)
WURZBURGER PERKUSSIONS
ENSEMBLE. Siegfried Fink, director.

THO MTH 124
PERCUSSION ENSEMBLE SIEGFRIED
FINK.

-**Conga Negro**
THO MTH 149
PERCUSSION ENSEMBLE SIEGFRIED
FINK.

-**Improvisation und Umkehrung**
(1967)
For vibraphone.
AUD 63 407
AXEL FRIES (vibraphone).

-**Marcha del Tambor**
THO MTH 124
PERCUSSION ENSEMBLE SIEGFRIED
FINK.

-**Plaisanterie - Quatre Etudes pour**
Percussion
Thorofon CTH 2003 (Compact Disc)
WURZBURGER PERKUSSIONS
ENSEMBLE. Siegfried Fink, director.

THO MTH 124
PERCUSSION ENSEMBLE SIEGFRIED
FINK.

Trio PA-4010
TOMOYUKI OKADA, TATSUO SASAKI,
ISAO MORIYAMA, and KAZUKI
MOMOSE (percussion).

-**Rondell I** **(1971)**
For percussion and orchestra
THO MTH 183
SIEGFRIED FINK, BERND KREMLING,
WOLFGANG SCHNEIDER, and JOACHIM
SPONSEL (percussion).

-**Tangents** **(1977)**
Cal CAL 30 492
WURZBURG MUSIC SCHOOL
PERCUSSION ENSEMBLE.

-**Timing**
For percussion.
THO MTH 183
SIEGFRIED FINK, BERND KREMLING,
WOLFGANG SCHNEIDER, and JOACHIM
SPONSEL (percussion).

-**Top-capi** **(1980)**
Cal CAL 30 492
WURZBURG MUSIC SCHOOL
PERCUSSION ENSEMBLE.

-**Vibracussion**
For vibraphone and percussion
instruments.
THO MTH 149
PERCUSSION ENSEMBLE SIEGFRIED
FINK.

-**Zulu Welcome**
SST (Sound Star - Tonprod) 0 164
PERCUSSION ENSEMBLE OF THE
BADISCHEN CONSERVATORY.

FISSINGER, ALFRED (1925-)

-**Suite for Marimba** **(1950)**
BIS LP-149
RAINER KUISMA (marimba).

Epic P-17808
VIDA CHENOWETH (marimba).

Studio 4 Productions S4P - R101
KAREN ERVIN (marimba).

FITT, ROBERT

-**Mallets in Wonderland**
King Records K-28C-165
MAKOTO ARUGA PERCUSSION
ENSEMBLE.

FONVILLE, JOHN

-**An Afternoon with Anron at the**
Cafe
TR^2 001
MICHAEL UDOW (percussion) with
THE TONE ROAD RAMBLERS.

-**Proverbs/Converbs**
TR^2 001
MICHAEL UDOW (percussion) with
THE TONE ROAD RAMBLERS.

FOSS, LUKAS (1922-)

-**Echoi**
For percussion, cello, clarinet, and
piano.
Wergo 60040
JAN WILLIAMS (percussion).

-**Elytres**
For flute, violins, harp, piano, and
percussion.
Turnabout 34514
JAN WILLIAMS (percussion).

-The Fragments of Archilochos
For tenor, chorus, speaker,
mandolin, guitar, and percussion.
Wergo WER 60040
JAN WILLIAMS, EDWARD BURNHAM,
and LYNN HARBOLD (percussion).

-Music for Six
For percussion.
CRI S-413
UNIVERSITY OF BUFFALO
PERCUSSION ENSEMBLE.

-Ni Bruitt Ni Vitesse
For 2 pianos and 2 percussionists.
Turnabout 34514
JAN WILLIAMS (percussion).

-Non-Improvisation
For piano, cello, clarinet, and
percussion.
Wergo WER 60040
JAN WILLIAMS (percussion).

-Paradigm
For high, middle, and low
instruments, electric guitar, and
percussion.
Turnabout 34514
JAN WILLIAMS (percussion).

-Percussion Quartet
New World Records NW 330
THE NEW MUSIC CONSORT

-Solo Observed
For piano, cello, vibraphone, and
electric organ.
Gramavision 7005
RICHARD FITZ (vibraphone).

FRAZEUR, THEODORE (1929-   )

-Four Sea Fragments
For clarinet and percussion.
Grenadilla 1042
THEODORE FRAZEUR (percussion).

-Frieze
For violin and percussion.
Grenadilla 1042
THEODORE FRAZEUR (percussion).

-Three Irish Folk Songs (arr. Frazeur)
For flute and percussion.
CRS 8425

FRIEDMAN, DAVID

-Nyack
For marimba and vibraphone.
Marimba Productions MP-002
DOUBLE IMAGE (DAVID FRIEDMAN
and DAVE SAMUELS
(marimba/vibraphone).

FRIEDMAN, DAVID and SAMUELS, DAVE

-Carousel
For marimba and vibraphone.
Marimba Productions MP-002
DOUBLE IMAGE (DAVID FRIEDMAN
and DAVE SAMUELS
(marimba/vibraphone).

FRIES, AXEL (1954-   )

-Eisblumen (1982)
For percussion instruments.
AUD 63 407
AXEL FRIES (percussion).

-L'Hippocampe (1981)
For vibraphone.
AUD 63 407
AXEL FRIES (vibraphone).

FRITSCH, JOHANNES G. (1941-   )

-Concerto Battuto
THO MTH 183
SIEGFRIED FINK, BERND KREMLING,
WOLFGANG SCHNEIDER, and JOACHIM
SPONSEL (percussion).

FUJITA, MASANORI

-Ichinogotoshi II
For percussion.
Camerata Tokyo CMT-1010
SUMIRE YOSHIHARA (percussion).

FUKUSHI, NORIO

-Ground I (1976)
For solo percussion.
Camerata Tokyo CMT-1027
SUMIRE YOSHIHARA (percussion).

G

GABER, HARLEY (1943-   )

-Ludus Primus
For two flutes and vibraphone.
CRI SD-299
RAYMOND DesROCHES (vibraphone).

GARDO, RYSZARD (1923-   )

-Triptych
For percussion.
MUZA SXL 0809

GARLAND, PETER (1953-   )

-Apple Blossom (1972)
Opus One 22
BLACKEARTH PERCUSSION GROUP.

GAUGER, THOMAS

-Portico
Second Hearing GS 9008 (Compact Disc)
UNIVERSITY OF OKLAHOMA
PERCUSSION ENSEMBLE.

GEAY, GÉRARD

-Puzzle
For marimba.
Denon 35C37-7279 (Compact Disc)
KEIKO ABE (marimba).

GENZMER, HARALD

-Capriccio
For marimba.
AUL PRE 68 521
HERMANN GSCHWENDTNER
(marimba).

-Konzert
For piano and percussion.
AUL PRE 68 521
HERMANN GSCHWENDTNER
(percussion).

-Sonate
For vibraphone.
AUL PRE 68 521
HERMANN GSCHWENDTNER
(vibraphone).

GERBER, RENÉ (1908-   )

-Three Poems
For contralto, piano, and percussion.
Gallo 30-348

-Three Spanish Visions
For contralto, wind quintet, piano
four hands, and percussion.
Gallo 30-348

GERSHWIN, GEORGE (1898-1937)

-Prelude II (from **Preludes for Piano**)
OMR 1001
ED HARTMAN (marimba).

GIBSON, ROBERT

-Notturno
For piccolo, clarinet, viola, cello,
piano, and percussion.
Spectrum 144

GIDEON, MIRIAM (1906-   )

-Questions on Nature (1965)
For voice, oboe, piano, and
percussion.
CRI SD-343
B. JEKOFSKY (percussion).

-Rhymes from the Hill (1968)
For mezzo-soprano, clarinet,
violoncello, and marimba.
CRI SD-286
RAYMOND DesROCHES (marimba).

GILBERT, PIA (1921 -   )

-Transmutations
Protone 150
SCOTT SHEPHERD (percussion).

GINASTERA, ALBERTO (1916-1983)

-Cantata para América Mágica
For dramatic soprano and 53
percussion   instruments.
Columbia Materworks ML-5847
LOS ANGELES PERCUSSION ENSEMBLE.

CSP AMS-6447
LOS ANGELES PERCUSSION ENSEMBLE.

GLANVILLE-HICKS, PEGGY (1912-   )

-Sonata for Piano and Percussion
(1952)
Columbia ML-4990
NEW YORK PERCUSSION GROUP.

GOODMAN, SAUL (1906-   )

-Scherzo for Percussion
King Records K-28C-165
MAKOTO ARUGA PERCUSSION
ENSEMBLE.

-Timpiana
SST 0 164
PERCUSSION ENSEMBLE OF THE
BADISCHEN CONSERVATORY.

GOODRICH, LORRAINE

-Octave Etude in D minor
Epic P-17808
VIDA CHENOWETH (marimba).

GOSSELIN, ANDRE

-Rag 'n' Roll
Croissant CRO-2001
REPERCUSSION.

GOTTLIEB, GORDON and GOTTLIEB, JAY

-Graines Gémellaires
For percussion and piano.
Auvidis AV 4831
GORDON GOTTLIEB (percussion).

-Traversées
For percussion and piano.
Auvidis AV 4831
GORDON GOTTLIEB (percussion).

GRAVES, MEL (1946-   )

-Cave Dwellers
For percussion, bassoon, steel drums,
and contrabass.
1750 Arch 1780

-Coral Reef
For percussion, bassoon, steel drums,
and contrabass.
1750 Arch 1780

-Energy Fields
For percussion, bassoon, steel drums,
and contrabass.
1750 Arch 1780

-Ladder to the Moon
For percussion, bassoon, steel drums,
and contrabass.
1750 Arch 1780

-Sky Above Clouds
For percussion, bassoon, steel drums,
and contrabass.
1750 Arch 1780

-Watercourse
For percussion, bassoon, steel drums,
and contrabass.
1750 Arch 1780

**GREEN, GEORGE HAMILTON (1893-
1970)**

-Caprice. Op. 14
Conservatory 7101 M
GEORGE HAMILTON GREEN
(xylophone).

-Charleston Capers
Conservatory 7101 M
GEORGE HAMILTON GREEN
(xylophone).

Hungaroton HCD 12855 (Compact
Disc)
AMADINDA PERCUSSION GROUP.

Hungaroton SLPD 12800
AMADINDA PERCUSSION GROUP.

- Chromatic Foxtrot
Mercury (Golden Imports) SRI 75108
THE EASTMAN MARIMBA BAND.

-Concert Waltz in G
Conservatory 7101 M
GEORGE HAMILTON GREEN
(xylophone).

-Cross Corners
Conservatory 7101 M
GEORGE HAMILTON GREEN
(xylophone).

Mercury (Golden Imports) SRI 75108
THE EASTMAN MARIMBA BAND.

Umbrella UMB DD-2
NEXUS. (arr. **Bob Becker**)

-**Fluffy Ruffles**
Second Hearing GS 9008 (Compact
Disc)
UNIVERSITY OF OKLAHOMA
PERCUSSION ENSEMBLE.

-**Jovial Jasper**
Conservatory 7101 M
GEORGE HAMILTON GREEN
(xylophone).

Hungaroton HCD 12855 (Compact
Disc)
AMADINDA PERCUSSION GROUP.

Hungaroton SLPD 12800
AMADINDA PERCUSSION GROUP.

Mercury (Golden Imports) SRI 75108
THE EASTMAN MARIMBA BAND.

Umbrella UMB DD-2
NEXUS. (arr. **Bob Becker**)

-**Log Cabin Blues**
Hungaroton HCD 12855 (Compact
Disc)
AMADINDA PERCUSSION GROUP.

Hungaroton SLPD 12800
AMADINDA PERCUSSION GROUP.

Mercury (Golden Imports) SRI 75108
THE EASTMAN MARIMBA BAND.

Umbrella UMB DD-2
NEXUS. (arr. **Bob Becker**)

-**Ragtime Robin.**
Conservatory 7101 M
GEORGE HAMILTON GREEN
(xylophone).

Umbrella UMB DD-2
NEXUS. (arr. **Bob Becker**)

-**Rainbow Ripples**
Conservatory 7101 M
GEORGE HAMILTON GREEN
(xylophone).

Mercury (Golden Imports) SRI 75108
THE EASTMAN MARIMBA BAND.

Umbrella UMB DD-2
NEXUS. (arr. **Bob Becker**)

-**Stop Time**
Umbrella UMB DD-2
NEXUS. (arr. **Bob Becker**)

-**Triplets**
Conservatory 7101 M
GEORGE HAMILTON GREEN
(xylophone).

Mercury (Golden Imports) SRI 75108
THE EASTMAN MARIMBA BAND.

Umbrella UMB DD-2
NEXUS. (arr. **Bob Becker**)

-**The Whistler**
Mercury (Golden Imports) SRI 75108
THE EASTMAN MARIMBA BAND.

Umbrella UMB DD-2
NEXUS. (arr. **Bob Becker**)

GREEN, JOE

-**Xylophonia**
Umbrella UMB DD-2
NEXUS. (arr. **Bob Becker**)

GRIFFITH, MARSHALL (1953-)

-**Plagal Alternations**
For timpani and percussion.
Crystal S-533
CLOYD DUFF (timpani) and DONALD
MILLER (percussion).

GUARNIERI, CAMARGO (1907-)

-**Concerto for String Orchestra and
Percussion**
USP LP-002
DJALMA COLANERI, CARLOS TARCHA,
and RICHARD dos SANTOS
(percussion).

GUINJOAN, JOAN (1935-)

-**Cinco Estudios**
For 2 pianos and percussion
instruments.
THO MTH 218
SIEGFRIED FINK and XAVIER JOAQUIN
(percussion).

-**Prisma**
For vibraphone, marimba, and piano.
Thorofon CTH 2003 (Compact Disc)
WURZBURGER PERKUSSIONS
ENSEMBLE.   Siegfried Fink, director.

THO MTH 218
SIEGFRIED FINK and XAVIER JOAQUIN
(percussion).

-**Tension-Relax** (1974)
For percussion.
AUD 63 407
AXEL FRIES (percussion).

H

HACHIMURA, YOSHIO (1938-   )

-**Ahania**
For marimba.
Denon 30C0-1729 (Compact Disc)
KEIKO ABE (marimba).

Denon 35C37-7279 (Compact Disc)
KEIKO ABE (marimba).

-**Breathing Field, Op. 15** (1981/2)
For flute, clarinet, harp, piano, and
percussion.
Camerata Tokyo CMT-1093
YASUNORI YAMAGUCHI
(percussion).

-**Constellation, Op. 5** (1969)
For violin, piano, tubular bells, and
vibraphone.
Camerata Tokyo CMT-1092
SUMIRE YOSHIHARA (vibraphone)
and YASUNORI YAMAGUCHI (tubular
bells).

-**Dolcissima Mia Vita, Op.16** (1981)
For metallic percussion instruments.
Camerata Tokyo CMT-1093
SUMIRE YOSHIHARA (percussion).

CBS Sony 32DC-1009 (Compact Disc)
SUMIRE YOSHIHARA (percussion).

-**On Hour at Every One Breathe -**
Concerto for 8 soloists Op. 3 (1960)
For flute, clarinet, tenor sax, violin,
soprano, vibraphone, and
percussion.
Camerata Tokyo CMT-1091
ATSUSHI SUGAHARA (vibraphone);
YASUNORU YAMAGUCHI and SUMIRE
YOSHIHARA (percussion).

HAKIM, TALIB RASUL (1940-   )

-**Placements**
For five percussionists and piano.
Folkways 33903

HALFFTER, CRISTOBAL (1930-   )

-**Noche Pasiva del Sentido**
For soprano and percussion.
CHR SCK 70 356
JOHN DVORACHEK (percussion).

HALL, REX T.

-**March Humoresque**
King Records K-28C-165
MAKOTO ARUGA PERCUSSION
ENSEMBLE.

HALLER, HANS PETER (1929-   )

-**Harvest Work**
For double bass and percussion.
CHR SCK 70 356
MARKUS STECKELER (percussion).

HALPERIN, ART (see: SLAWSON, BRIAN)

HAMBRAEUS, BENGT (1928-   )

-**Konstellationen - Nr. 4**
For organ and percussion.
CHR SCGLX 73 971
SIEGFRIED FINK (percussion).

HAMILTON, TOM (In cooperation with
RICH O'DONNELL and J.D. PARRAN)

-**Crimson Sterling** (1973)
SOMRATH Records KH 130 Stereo

-**Formal and Informal Music** (1980)
SOMRATH Records KH 130 Stereo

HAMM, CHARLES

-Canto 1963
For soprano, speaker, flute, clarinet, sax, prepared piano, and tape.
HEL (Heliodor) H-25 047

HANDEL, GEORGE FRIDERIC (1685-1759)

-Return of the Queen of Sheba
(From Solomon)
CBS Records M-39704 Stereo
BRIAN SLAWSON (keyboard percussion).

CBS MK-39704 (Compact Disc)
BRIAN SLAWSON (keyboard percussion).

HANNA, STEPHEN (1950-   )

-Sonic Sauce
For percussion.
Crystal 140
SONIC BOOM PERCUSSION ENSEMBLE.

HANUS, JAN (1915-   )

-Sonata Seria
For violin and percussion.
Serenus 12083
OLDRICH SATAVA (percussion).

-Two Movements for Timpani and Tape
Serenus 12083
PETR SPRUNK (percussion).

HARBISON, JOHN (1938-   )

-The Flower-Fed Buffaloes (1976)
For clarinet, tenor saxophone, violin, cello, contrabass, piano, and percussion.
Nonesuch H-71366

HARRIS, ROY (1898-1979)

-Concerto
For amplified piano, brass, basses, and percussion.
Varese/Sarabande 81085

-Fantasy
For organ, brass, and timpani.
Varese/Sarabande 81085

HARRISON, LOU (1917-   ) (see also: CAGE, JOHN)

-Canticle No. 1
For sistrum, tambourine, 3 wood blocks, 3 high bells, gourd rattle, 3 dragon's mouths, 3 large glass bells, wood rattle, 3 claybells, 3 cowbells, morache, windbell, triangle, suspended cymbals, brake drum, thundersheet, bell, gong, tam-tam, 3 high drums, 3 low drums, and 3 muted gongs.
Mainstream Records MS/5011
RAYMOND DesROCHES, MICHAEL ROSENBERG, EDWARD CORNELIUS, WARREN SMITH, and GEORGE BOBERG (percussion).

-Canticle No. 3
Urania UX-106
AMERICAN PERCUSSION SOCIETY.
Paul Price, conductor.

-Concerto for Organ with Percussion Orchestra
Crystal S-858
LOS ANGELES PERCUSSION ENSEMBLE.

-Concerto for Violin with Percussion Orchestra (Koncherto Por La Violino Kun Perkuta Orkestro)
Crystal S-853
LOS ANGELES PERCUSSION ENSEMBLE.

Turnabout QTV-S 34653
THE EASTMAN PERCUSSION ENSEMBLE.

-Concerto No. 1 for Flute and Percussion (1939)
BIS LP-272 (D)
KROUMATA PERCUSSION ENSEMBLE.

BIS CD-272 (Compact Disc)
KROUMATA PERCUSSION ENSEMBLE.

-Fugue for Percussion (1941)
Opus One 22
BLACKEARTH PERCUSSION GROUP.

-Song of Queztalcoatl (1941)
For 5 wood blocks, 5 dragon's
mouths, 5 bells, sistrums, maracas. 5
suspended brake drums, 5 muted
brake drums, 5 cowbells, rattle,
snare drum, guiro, windglass,
triangle, gong, tam-tam, 5 tom-toms,
and contrabass drum.
Orion 642
PRICE PERCUSSION ENSEMBLE.

Period Records SPL 743
PHILIP BROWN, PAUL PRICE,
WARREN SMITH, and MICHAEL
COLGRASS (percussion).

-Suite for Percussion
CRI S252
MANHATTAN PERCUSSION ENSEMBLE.
Paul Price, conductor.

HARSANY, TIBOR (1898-1954)

-Histoire du Petit Tailleur (1939)
For 7 instruments and percussion.
Angel S-36357

HARTMAN, ED

-First Flight
OMR 1001
ED HARTMAN (percussion).

-Improvisation for Klaus
OMR 1001
ED HARTMAN (percussion).

-The River
OMR 1001
ED HARTMAN (percussion).

HASHAGEN, KLAUS (1924-)

-Meditation
For solo percussion.
COLO 0 557
SIEGFRIED FINK (percussion).

-Mobile Szenen I
COLO 0 557
SIEGFRIED FINK (percussion).

-Percussion IV/V
THO MTH 183
SIEGFRIED FINK, BERND KREMLING,
WOLFGANG SCHNEIDER, and JOACHIM
SPONSEL (percussion).

-Percussion VI
COLO 0 557
SIEGFRIED FINK (percussion).

HASSELL, JOHN (1937-)

-Vernal Equinox (1976)
For concrete sounds, percussion, and
electronics.
Lovely LML-1021

HAUFRECHT, HERBERT (1909-)

-Symphony for brass and timpani
CRI SD-192

HAYDN, FRANZ JOSEPH (1732-1809)

-Divertimento
For marimba and vipraphone.
THO MTH 149
PERCUSSION ENSEMBLE SIEGFRIED
FINK.

HEIDEN, BERNARD

-Four Movements
For saxophone quartet and timpani.
Golden Crest CRS-4224
GEORGE GABER (timpani).

HEIDER, WERNER (1930-)

-Galerie
For percussion quartet.
Wergo WER 60123
STEFAN GAGELMANN, JÜRGEN
FRIEDEL, MATTHIAS JAKOB, and
ELMAR KOLB (percussion).

Wergo WER 60123-50 (Compact Disc)
STEFAN GAGELMANN, JÜRGEN
FRIEDEL, MATTHIAS JAKOB, and
ELMAR KOLB (percussion).

-Katalog fur einen Vibraphonspieler
COLO 0 628
SIEGFRIED FINK (vibraphone).

HEISS, JOHN (1928-)

-Capriccio
For flute, clarinet, and percussion.
CRI S-486
FRANK EPSTEIN (percussion).

HELBLE, RAYMOND

-Diabolic Variations
Second Hearing GS 9008
UNIVERSITY OF OKLAHOMA
PERCUSSION ENSEMBLE.

HELLERMAN, WILLIAM (1939-)

-Ek-Stasis II (1970)
For amplified piano, percussion, and
electronic tape.
CRI SD-299
MICHAEL LEVENSON (percussion).

HENNAGIN, MICHAEL

-Duo Chopinesque
Second Hearing GS 9008
UNIVERSITY OF OKLAHOMA
PERCUSSION ENSEMBLE.

HENZE, HANS WERNER (1926-)

-El Cimarrón
For baritone, flute, guitar, and
percussion.
DG 2707 050
STOMU YAMASH'TA (percussion).

-Five Scenes from the Snow Country
For marimba solo.
Wergo WER 60123
FRANZ LANG (marimba).

Wergo WER 60123-50 (Compact Disc)
FRANZ LANG (marimba).

-Prison Song
Decca SLA (O) - 1032
STOMU YAMASH'TA (percussion).

L'Oiseau-Lyre DSLO 1
STOMU YAMASH'TA (percussion).

**HERTEL, JOHANN WILHELM (1727-
1789)**

**-Concerto for 8 kettledrums, winds,
and strings. (Konzert für 8 Paüken,
Bläser, und Streicher)**
SCHW VMS 2066
WERNER THÄRICHEN or NICHOLAS
BARDACH (kettledrums).

Schwann Musica Mundi CD 11066
(Compact Disc)
WERNER THÄRICHEN or NICHOLAS
BARDACH (kettledrums).

HERVIG, RICHARD (1917-)

**-Suite for Vibraphone and Marimba
(1981)**
U. of Iowa Press 8319
STEVEN SCHICK (vibraphone and
marimba).

HEUSSENSTAMM, GEORGE (1926-)

-Tetralogue
For 4 clarinets and percussion.
WIM 7
OWEN, MICHALSKY, and CAMPO
(percussion).

HILLER, LEJAREN (1924-)

-An Avalanche
For pitchman, prima donna, player
piano, percussionist, and pre-
recorded play-back text.
1968 Heliodor 25-49006

-Machine Music (1964)
For piano, percussion, and tape.
Turnabout TV-S 34536
JEFFREY KOWALSKY (percussion).

HILLER, WILFRIED (1941-)

-An diesen heutigen Tage
For voice and 4 percussionists.
Wergo WER 4 004
PETER WEINER, KARL PEINKOFER,
ANDREAS VONDERTHANN, and RIK
DEMEURICY (percussion).

-Katalog IV (1976-79)
For percussion.
Wergo WER 60123
THILO BERG, WILLI FORSTER, ELMAR
KOLB, and MICHAEL LANG
(percussion).

Wergo WER 60123-50 (Compact Disc)
THILO BERG, WILLI FORSTER, ELMAR
KOLB, and MICHAEL LANG
(percussion).

HISAISHI, JOE

-Flash-Bach
For two percussionists.
Nippon Columbia YF-7019 ND
MIDORI TAKADA and YOJI SADANARI
(percussion).

-Mkwaju Suite
For keyboard, computer
programming, and percussion.
Nippon Columbia YF-7019 B
MIDORI TAKADA, YOJI SADANARI,
and JUNKO ARASE (percussion).

-Pulse In My Mind
For piano and percussion.
Nippon Columbia YF-7019 B
MIDORI TAKADA, YOJI SADANARI,
and JUNKO ARASE (percussion).

HODKINSON, SYDNEY (1934-   )

-Drawings: Set No.1
For percussion quartet.
Trio PA-4010
KAZUKI MOMOSE, MITSUAKI
IMAMURA, SEIICHIRO SADANARI,
and TOMOYUKI OKADA (percussion).

-The Edge of the Olde One
For electric english horn, strings,
and percussion.
Grenadilla 1048
EASTMAN MUSICA NOVA.

-Two Structures (1957)
For percussion ensemble.
CRS 6
UNIVERSITY OF ILLINOIS
PERCUSSION ENSEMBLE.

HØJSGAARD, ERIK (1954-   )

-Cendrée (1979)
For solo percussion.
Paula Denmark 35
F. HANSEN (percussion).

HONEGGER, ARTHUR (1892-1955)

-Pacific 231 (Mouement
Symphonique No. 1) (1924)
ARA 8035
Birmingham Symphony - Frémaux,
conductor.

Erato NUM 75254 (D)
Bavarian Radio Symphony - Dutoit,
conductor.

London STS5-15591
Suisse Romande - Ansermet,
conductor.

HOOD, BOYDE W. (1939-   )

-Pange Lingua
Golden Crest S-4087

HORWOOD, MICHAEL (1947-   )

-Piece Percussionique No. 5
Opus One 61
GERALD HESLIP and JOHN BROWNELL
(percussion).

HOVHANESS, ALAN (1911-   )

-Fantasy on Japanese Woodprints,
Op. 211
For xylophone and orchestra.
CBS M-34537
YOICHI HIRAOKA (xylophone).

-Firdausi, Op. 252
For clarinet, harp, and percussion.
Grenadilla GS-1008
NEAL BOYAR (percussion).

-Khaidis, Op. 91
For piano, four trumpets, and
percussion.
M-G-M Records E-3160
Poseidon 1011

-Koke No Niwa
For english horn, harp, timpani,
tam-tam, glockenspiel, and marimba.
CRI S-186
ELDEN BAILEY and WALTER
ROSENBERGER (percussion).

-October Mountain (1942)
For marimba, glockenspiel, timpani,
tenor and bass drums, gong, and
tam-tam.
Urania UR 134
MANHATTAN PERCUSSION ENSEMBLE.
Paul Price, conductor.

-Requiem and Resurrection
For brass and percussion.
Poseidon Society 1002

-**Suite for Violin, Piano, and Percussion**
Columbia CML-5179
ELDEN BAILEY (percussion).

-**Tzaikerk**
For solo violin, flute, drums, and string orchestra.
Crystal S-800
MITCHELL PETERS (drums).

Crystal CD-801 (Compact Disc)
MITCHELL PETERS (drums).

HUBER, NICOLAUS A. (1939-   )

-**Dasselbe ist nicht dasselbe** (1978)
For snare drum.
HM DMR 1022/24
EDITH SALMEN (snare drum).

HULICK, TERRY

-**Rondino**
For percussion quartet.
Golden Crest CR-4016
ITHACA PERCUSSION ENSEMBLE.
Warren Benson, director.

HUMMEL, BERTHOLD (1925-   )

-**Fresken '70**
For percussion quartet.
Cal CAL 30 492
WURZBURG MUSIC SCHOOL PERCUSSION ENSEMBLE. Siegfried Fink, conductor.

HUSA, KAREL (1921-   )

-**Concerto for Percussion and Winds**
Golden Crest 5066
MICHIGAN STATE PERCUSSION ENSEMBLE.

I

IBARRA, FEDERICO

-**La Chute des Anges'** (1983)
For percussion.
UNAM Records
ORQUESTA DE PERCUSION DE LA UNIVERSIDAD NACIONAL AUTONOMA DE MEXICO (UNAM).

IBARRONDO, FELIX (1943-   )

-**Sino** (1981)
For soprano, mixed chorus, brass, and percussion.
HM 5132

ICHIYANAGI, TOSHI (1933-   )

-**Arrangements**
For percussion player.
RCA RDCE-9
SUMIRE YOSHIHARA (percussion).

-**Paganini Personal** (1982)
For marimba and piano.
Camerata Tokyo CMT-4016
HIROYUKI IWAKI (marimba).

-**Time in Tree, Time in Water**
For percussion.
CBS Sony 32DC-1009 (Compact Disc)
SUMIRE YOSHIHARA (percussion).

IFUKUBE, AKIRA (1914-   )

-**Lauda Concertata,** (1979)
For marimba and orchestra.
Fontec FONC-5031
KEIKO ABE (marimba) with the SHINSEI NIHON SYMPHONY ORCHESTRA, Kazuo Yamada, conductor.

IKEBE, SHIN-ICHIRO (1943-   )

-**Monovalence I**
For marimba.
Denon 30C0-1727 (Compact Disc)
KEIKO ABE (marimba).

Denon 35C37-7279 (Compact Disc)
KEIKO ABE (marimba).

Nippon Columbia Co., Ltd. OQ-7466
KEIKO ABE (marimba).

-**Monovalence VI**
For mitla.
Japan Federation of Composers JFC R-8302
JUNKO ARASE (mitla).

IKENO, SEI (1931-)

-Evocation
For marimba, six trombones and six percussionists.
Japan Federation of Composers JFC-8001
TAKAYA NAKATANI (marimba); MAKOTO ARUGA, AKIYOSHI ADACHI, TSUNENORI MOCHIMARU, HIROYOSHI INUMA, SHIGERU MAEDA, NOBUYUKI HIRAO (percussion).

ISHII, MAKI (1936-)

-Drifting Island, Op. 37 (1979)
For 17-string koto and percussion.
Camerata Tokyo CMT-1059
SUMIRE YOSHIHARA (percussion).

-Marimbastück.
For marimba and two percussionists.
Candide/Vox Records CE 31051
KEIKO ABE (marimba); MAKOTO ARUGA and HIDEHIKO SATO (percussion).

Denon 30C0-1729 (Compact Disc)
KEIKO ABE (marimba); MAKOTO ARUGA and HIDEHIKO SATO (percussion).

-Search in Gray II
For solo percussion and tape.
Camerata Tokyo CMT-1010
SUMIRE YOSHIHARA (percussion).

-Sen-Ten (1971)
For percussion and electronic sounds.
Toshiba/EMI TCM-006
MAKOTO ARUGA (percussion).

-Synkretism I (1973)
For marimba and five instrumental groups.
Denon 38C37 7280 (Compact Disc)
KEIKO ABE (marimba) with the TOKYO QUINTET.

J

JANSON, ALFRED

-Canon
For chamber orchestra and magnetic band.
1964 Limelight LS-86061
PER ERIK THORSEN (percussion).

Phillips France - 836 896 DSY

JAPANESE FOLK SONG

-Lullaby of Itsuki
Denon OF-7163-ND
KEIKO ABE (marimba) and WALTER VAN HAUWE (recorder).

Denon 33C37-7393 (Compact Disc)
KEIKO ABE (marimba) and WALTER VAN HAUWE (recorder).

-Lullaby of Shimabara
Denon OF-7163-ND
KEIKO ABE (marimba) and WALTER VAN HAUWE (recorder).

Denon 33C37-7393 (Compact Disc)
KEIKO ABE (marimba) and WALTER VAN HAUWE (recorder).

-Kariboshi Kiri Uta
Denon OF-7163-ND
KEIKO ABE (marimba) and WALTER VAN HAUWE (recorder).

Denon 33C37-7393 (Compact Disc)
KEIKO ABE (marimba) and WALTER VAN HAUWE (recorder).

JENEY, ZOLTAN (1943-)

-To Apollo (Cantata)
For chorus, english horn, organ, and cymbals.
Hungaroton 12366

JENNI, DONALD (1937-)

-Cucumber Music (1969)
For flute, piano, and percussion.
CRI S-324
PARSONS (percussion).

JOEL, BILLY

-**Just The Way You Are** (arr. R. Gipson)
For percussion ensemble.
Second Hearing GS 9008
UNIVERSITY OF OKLAHOMA
PERCUSSION ENSEMBLE.

JOHNSON, CHARLES

-**Dill Pickles**
Umbrella UMB DD-2
NEXUS. (arr. Bob Becker)

JOHNSON, GREGG

-**Lemon Sisters**
CMP Records CMP 31 CS
REPERCUSSION UNIT

JOHNSON, TOM (1939-   )

-**Nine Bells**
For alarm bells.
India Navigation 3023

JOHNSTON, BENJAMIN (1926-   )

-**Dirge** (1952)
CRS 6   University of Illinois School
of Music Custom Recording Series
UNIVERSITY OF ILLINOIS
PERCUSSION ENSEMBLE. Jack
McKenzie, conductor.

JOLIVET, ANDRÉ (1905-1974)

-**Suite en Concert**
For flute and percussion.
BIS LP-272 (D)
KROUMATA PERCUSSION ENSEMBLE.

BIS CD-272
KROUMATA PERCUSSION ENSEMBLE.

3 RCA CRL3-1429
CASADESUS, DROUET, MASSON,
FRANCOIS, PERCUSSION ENSEMBLE.

Teldec 642364

Thorofon CTH 2003 (Compact Disc)
WURZBURGER PERKUSSIONS
ENSEMBLE. Siegfried Fink, director.

THO MTH 149
PERCUSSION ENSEMBLE SIEGFRIED
FINK.

JONES, DANIEL (1912-   )

-**Sonata for Three Unaccompanied Kettledrums**
Argo ZRG 772
TRISTAN FRY (kettledrums).

Classics for Pleasure CFP 40207
TRISTAN FRY (kettledrums)

JONES, JEFF (1944-   )

-**Ambiance, (Quatre poemes de Samuel Beckett)**
For soprano, flute, piccolo, oboe,
english horn, bassoon, horn,
trumpet, trombone, violin, cello,
piano, celesta, harpsichord, harp,
and percussion.
Nonesuch 71302
RAYMOND DesROCHES, RICHARD FITZ,
HOWARD Van HYNING, CLAIRE
HELDRICH, GORDON GOTTLIEB, and
JOSEPH PASSARO (percussion).

JOPLIN, SCOTT (1868-1917)

-**Joplin Rag Meddley** (arr. Holmgren)
Mark Records MES 38080
THE 1978 P.A.S.I.C. MARIMBA
ORCHESTRA.

K

KABELAC, MILOSLAV (1908-1979)

-**8 Inventions, Op. 45**
Phillips 836.990 DSY
LES PERCUSSIONS DE STRASBOURG.

Phillips Stereo 6718 040
LES PERCUSSIONS DE STRASBOURG.

Phillips 32 CD 3063 (Compact Disc)
LES PERCUSSIONS DE STRASBOURG.

-**Scherzo**
Golden Crest 4145
UNIVERSITY OF MICHIGAN
PERCUSSION ENSEMBLE. Charles
Owen, conductor.

KAEGI, WERNER

-Gioco e Musica
CTS 44
JACQUES AUBERT (percussion).

KAGEL, MAURICIO (1932-)

-Match for Three Players
For two violoncellos and percussion.
DGG 137 006
CHRISTOPH CASKEL (percussion).

-Transición II
For piano, percussion, and two
magnetic tapes.
Limelight LS 86048

Mainstream 5003
CHRISTOPH CASKEL (percussion).

Time S/8001
CHRISTOPH CASKEL (percussion).

KAKO, TAKASHI

-Horoscope
For percussion.
Camerata Tokyo CMT-1086
SUMIRE YOSHIHARA (percussion).

KALMAR, LASZLO (1931-)

-Anera (1977)
Hungaroton SLPX 12065
GABOR KOSA (percussion).

KANNO, YOSHIHIRO (1953-)

-Stratosphere (1978)
For piano, harp, contrabass, and
percussion.
Japan Federation of Composers JFC-
8003
KOHYA NAKATANI (percussion).

-The Four Seasons in Resonance (12
Months of Japan)
Denon (Nippon Columbia Co., Ltd.)
38C37-7042 (Compact Disc)
TOMOYUKI OKADA PERCUSSION
ENSEMBLE.

KAPR, JAN (1914-)

-Ciphers
For piano, percussion, and
electronic sounds.
SVP (no catalog number)
I. KIESLICH (percussion).

-Concertino
For clarinet, cello, percussion, and
piano.
Serenus 12082

KARLINS, M. WILLIAM (1932-)

-Variations on "Obiter Dictum"
For amplified cello, piano, and
percussion.
CRI S-329

KAUFMAN, JEFFREY (1947-)

-In Time Past Remembered
For soprano, boy soprano, clarinet,
viola, piano, and percussion.
Grenadilla 1022

KEEZER, RONALD (1940-)

-For four percussionists
Crystal 140
SONIC BOOM PERCUSSION ENSEMBLE.

KELLER, HOMER (1915-)

-Interplay
For flute, horn, and percussion.
Advance 11

KELLY, ROBERT (1916-)

-Toccata (1959)
For marimba and percussion
ensemble.
CRS 6 University of Illinois School
of Music Custom Recording Series
UNIVERSITY OF ILLINOIS
PERCUSSION ENSEMBLE. Jack
McKenzie, conductor.

KESSNER, DANIEL (1946-   )

-**Equal II**
For piano, celesta, and 3
percussionists.
Orion 80397
TINTINNABULUM PERCUSSION
ENSEMBLE.

-**Equali VI**
Mark Records MES 38080
THE 1978 P.A.S.I.C. MARIMBA
ORCHESTRA.

KETTING, OTTO (1935-   )

-**Time Machine**
For winds and percussion.
Composers' Voice (DAVS) CV 7601

KEURIS, TRISTAN (1946-   )

-**Saxophone Concerto**
For alto saxophone, marimba,
glockenspiel, vibraphone, celesta,
piano, and strings.
DAVS 7374/4

KHACHATURIAN, ARAM (1903-1978)

-**Danse du Sabre**
Croissant CRO-2001
REPERCUSSION.

KIRCHNER, LEON (1919-   )

-**Toccata for Strings, Winds, and
Percussion**
Louisville S-683

KITAZUME, MICHIKO

-**Slapping Crossing**
For bass clarinet and percussion.
Camerata Tokyo CMT-1027
SUMIRE YOSHIHARA (percussion).

KNOX, CHARLES (1929-   )

-**Symphony for Brass and Percussion**
Golden Crest S-4085

KOBASHI, MINORU (1928-   )

-**Requiem (1980)**
For four percussionists.
Japan Federation of Composers JFC-
8103
SHIGEMITSU EISO, TOSHIYUKI
MATSUKURA, TAKASHI FUKUDA,
SATOSHI SAKAI (percussion).
(PERCUSSION GROUP '72).

KOBIALKA, DANIEL (1943-   )

-**Autumn Beyond**
For violins, biwa, and japanese bells.
1750 Arch 1795

-**Echoes of Secret Silence**
For strings, harp, and percussion.
1750 Arch 1792

KOHASHI, MINORU

-**A-Hun**
For percussion ensemble.
Cipango Corporation (Asia Record)
CC-5001
PERCUSSION GROUP '72.

-**Kijo (1975)**
For baritone and percussion.
Cipango Corporation (Asia Record)
CC-5001
PERCUSSION GROUP '72.

KOLB, BARBARA (1939-   )

-**Homage to Keith Jarret and Gary
Burton**
For flute and vibraphone.
CRS 8425

Leonarda 121
WILLIAM MOERSCH (vibraphone).

-**Looking for Claudio (1975)**
For soprano, baritone, guitar,
mandolin, and percussion.
CRI SD-361
GORDON GOTTLIEB (percussion).

-**Solitaire (1971)**
For piano, vibraphone, and tape.
Turnabout TV-S 34487
RICHARD FITZ (vibraphone)

-**Spring River Flowers Moon Night**
(1976)
For two pianos and percussion
ensemble.
CRI SD-361
BROOKLYN COLLEGE PERCUSSION
ENSEMBLE.   Barbara Kolb, conductor.

KOMORI, AKIHIRO (1931-   )

-**Psalterium for Percussionists**
(1973)
Japan Federation of Composers JFC-
7301
TOMOYUKI OKADA PERCUSSION
ENSEMBLE.

KONDO, JO (1947-   )

-**Standing** (1973)
For flute, marimba, and piano.
CP2 11
YASUNORI YAMAGUCHI (marimba).

-**Under the Umbrella** (1976)
For 25 cowbells and gong.
CP2 11
NEXUS.

KORTE, KARL (1928-   )

-**Gestures**
Golden Crest 4141
GEORGE FROCK (percussion).

-**Symmetrics**
For saxophone and percussion.
CRI S-431

KOSA, GABOR (1950-   )

-**2**
For vibraphone and xylorimba.
Hungaroton SLPX 12065
GABOR KOSA (vibraphone and
xylorimba).

KOSA, GYORGY (1897-   )

-**Divertimento** (1977)
Hungaroton SLPX 12065
GABOR KOSA (percussion).

KRAFT, LEO (1922-   )

-**Concerto No. 3**
For cello, winds, and percussion.
Serenus 12037

-**Line Drawings**
For flute and percussion.
Opus One 14
RICHARD FITZ (percussion).

KRAFT, WILLIAM (1923-   )

-**Des Imagistes**
For two readers and six
percussionists.
Delos DEL 254325 Q
WILLIAM KRAFT, KAREN ERVIN,
DALE ANDERSON, SCOTT HIGGINS,
MITCHELL PETERS and BARRY
SILVERMAN (percussion).

-**Double Trio** (1966)
For piano, prepared piano, amplified
guitar, tuba, and percussion.
Protone CSPR-163
RANEY (percussion).

-**Encounters I** (1975)
For solo percussion.
Protone CSPR-163
RANEY (percussion).

-**Encounters III**
For trumpet and percussion.
Avant Records AV-1003
MITCHELL PETERS (percussion).

-**Encounters IV: A Duel for Trombone**
and Percussion
Crystal 641
KAREN ERVIN (percussion).

-**Games: Collage No. 1**
For 22 brass and 4 percussion
soloists.
Angel S-1-36036
CHARLES De LANCEY, WALTER
GOODWIN, MITCHELL PETERS, AND
BARRY SILVERMAN (percussion).

-**Momentum**
For eight percussionists.
Crystal S-104
PACIFIC PERCUSSION ENSEMBLE.

Golden Crest 4145
UNIVERSITY OF MICHIGAN
PERCUSSION ENSEMBLE. Charles
Owen, conductor.

-Morris Dance
For percussion solo.
WIM 5
KAREN ERVIN (percussion).

-Nonet
For brass and percussion.
Crystal S-821
LOS ANGELES PERCUSSION ENSEMBLE.

-Suite for Percussion
Croissant CRO-2001
REPERCUSSION.

-Suite for Weatherkings (1958)
CRS 6   University of Illinois School
of Music Custom Recording Series
UNIVERSITY OF ILLINOIS
PERCUSSION ENSEMBLE. Jack
McKenzie, conductor.

-Theme and Variations
For four percussionists.
Crystal S-104
PACIFIC PERCUSSION ENSEMBLE.

-Triangles
For percussion soloist and chamber
orchestra.
Crystal S-104
BARRY SILVERMAN (percussion).

KRAMER, JONATHAN D.

-Five Studies On Six Notes (1980)
Opus One 80/81
THE PERCUSSION GROUP -
CINCINNATI.

-The Canons of Blackearth
Opus One 31
BLACKEARTH PERCUSSION GROUP.

KRAUS, PHIL

-Kriss-Kraus
Golden Crest CR 4004

KREISLER, FRITZ (1875-1962)

-Liebesfreud (arr. G. H. Green)
Conservatory 7101 M
GEORGE HAMILTON GREEN
(xylophone).

-Schon Rosmarin (arr. G.H. Green)
Conservatory 7101 M
GEORGE HAMILTON GREEN
(xylophone).

-Tambourin Chinois (arr. G. H. Green)
Studio 4 Productions S4P R-100
GORDON STOUT (marimba).

KRENEK, ERNST (1900-   )

-They Knew What They Wanted
For narrator, oboe, piano, and
percussion.
Orion 80380

KRUYF, TON de (1937-   )

-Seance
For percussion.
DAVS 7002
PERCUSSION GROUP AMSTERDAM.

KULESHA, GARY (1954-   )

-Angels
For marimba and pre-recorded tape.
Centredisques (Canada) WRC1-4951
BEVERLEY JOHNSTON (percussion).

KUNST, JOS (1936-   )

-No Time
For four clarinets, piano, and
percussion.
Composers' Voice (DAVS) 7475/3
ARIE VAN BEEK and WIM KOOPMAN
(percussion).

L

LACERDA, OSVALDO (1927-   )

-3 Brazilian Miniatures
Thorofon CTH 2003 (Compact Disc)
WURZBURGER PERKUSSIONS
ENSEMBLE. Siegfried Fink, director.

THO MTH 124
PERCUSSION ENSEMBLE SIEGFRIED
FINK.

LACHENMANN, HELMUT (1935-   )

-Air (1969)
For percussion solo and orchestra.
HM DMR 1013/15
MICHAEL RANTA - (solo percussion).

-Consolation (1967)
For 12 voices and percussion.
Wergo WER 60122

LAZAROF, HENRI (1932-   )

-Cadence III
For violin and two percussion
players.
Candide CE-31072
KENNETH WATSON and LARRY
BUNKER (percussion).

LEBIC, LOJZE (1934-   )

-Voices
For strings and percussion.
RTV Ljubljana LD 0706

LEEUW, TON de (1926-   )

-Midare
For marimba.
Composers' Voice (DAVS) CV 7602
MICHIKO TAKAHASHI (marimba).

CBS Sony 32 DC 5027 (Compact Disc)
MICHIKO TAKAHASHI (marimba).

LEMBA, ARTHUR

-Estonian Cradle Song (arr.
Wolfgang Pachla)
BIS LP-149
RAINER KUISMA (marimba).

LENTZ, DANIEL (1942-   )

-Lascaux
For 16 wine glasses.
Icon 5502

-Missa Umbrarum (1973)
For 8 voices and wine glasses.
New Albion NA-006

-O Ke-Wa (North American Eclipse)
(1974)
For 12 voices, bells, rasps, and
drums.
New Albion NA-006

LESEMANN, FREDERICK (1936-   )

-Sonata for Clarinet and Percussion
Crystal 641
KAREN ERVIN (percussion).

LEWIN-RICHTER, ANDRES

-Secuencia
For multiple percussion and tape.
HemisFerio Co., Spain (Seesaw Music
Corp., distributor - New York).
XAVIER JOAQUIN (percussion).

LEWIS, PETER TOD (1932-1982)

-Bricolage (1979)
For solo percussion and tape.
U. of Iowa Press 8319
STEVEN SCHICK (percussion).

LEWIS, ROBERT HALL (1926-   )

-Combinazioni II
For 8 percussionists and piano.
Orion 79363
EASTMAN PERCUSSION ENSEMBLE.

-Toccata for Solo Violin and
Percussion
CRI S-263
SAUL GOODMAN and WALTER
ROSENBERGER (percussion).

LIEBERMAN, ROLF (1910-   )

-Les Echanges
Thorofon CTH 2003 (Compact Disc)
WURZBURGER PERKUSSIONS
ENSEMBLE. Siegfried Fink, director.

THO MTH 124
PERCUSSION ENSEMBLE SIEGFRIED
FINK.

LLOYD WEBER, ANDREW (1948-   )

-Memory (arr. Richard Gipson)
Second Hearing GS 9008
UNIVERSITY OF OKLAHOMA
PERCUSSION ENSEMBLE.

LOCKLAIR, DAN (1949-   )

-Constellations (1980)
For organ and percussion.
Orion 85481
BROWN (percussion).

LOGAN, WENDELL

-Duo Exchanges
For clarinet, bass clarinet, and
percussion.
Orion 80373
MICHAEL ROSEN (percussion).

LOGOTHETIS, ANESTIS (1921-   )

-Katarakt
For percussion and orchestra.
Thorofon CTH 2003 (Compact Disc)
WURZBURGER PERKUSSIONS
ENSEMBLE. Siegfried Fink, director.

THO MTH 138
SIEGFRIED FINK, BERND KREMLING,
WOLFGANG SCHNEIDER, and JOACHIM
SPONSEL (percussion).

-Osculation
For bass clarinet, piano, and
percussion.
CAR 53 114

LoPRESTI, RONALD (1933-   )

-Sketch for Percussion (1956)
For xylophone, marimba, celeste,
timpani, snare drum, bass drum,
gong, piano, triangle, and suspended
cymbal.
Urania UR 134
MANHATTAN PERCUSSION ENSEMBLE.
Paul Price, conductor.

LOUDOVA, IVANA (1941-   )

-Concerto for Percussion, Organ, and
Wind Orchestra
AWS 103
AMERICAN WIND SYMPHONY.

LOUIE, ALEXINA (1949-   )

-Cadenzas
For marimba, glockenspiel,
vibraphone, and clarinet.
Centredisques (Canada) WRC1-4951
BEVERLEY JOHNSTON (percussion).

LOWENSTEIN, GUNILLA (1929-1981)

-Tellus Mater
For alto flute, marimba, and strings.
Caprice CAP 1266

LUNDQUIST, TORBJORN IWAN (1920-   )

-Sisu
For percussion sextet.
BIS LP-232 (D)
KROUMATA PERCUSSION ENSEMBLE.

BIS CD-232 (Compact Disc)
KROUMATA PERCUSSION ENSEMBLE.

Caprice CAP 1280
STOCKHOLM PERCUSSION ENSEMBLE.

LYLOFF, BENT (1930-   )

-Places
Cambridge 2824
COPENHAGEN PERCUSSION GROUP.

M

MacGREGOR, LAURIE (1951-   )

-Intrusion of the Hunter (1973-4)
For percussion.
CRI S-444
NEW JERSEY PERCUSSION ENSEMBLE.
Raymond DesRoches, conductor.

MACHE, FRANCOIS-BERNARD

-Temes Nevinbur
For 2 pianos, 2 percussionists, and
magnetic band.
Erato STU 70.860
JEAN PIERRE DROUET and SYLVIO
GUALDA (percussion).

MacINNIS, DONALD (1923-)

-Variations
For brass and percussion.
Golden Crest S-4084

MALEC, IVO (1925-)

-Actuor
HM 5134
LES PERCUSSIONS DE STRASBOURG.

MANDOLINI, RICARDO (1950-)

-Andromeda (1984)
For electronics and percussion.
Hungaroton SLPX-12809
SCHULZ (percussion).

MANN, ED

-Dream Toon
Robey Records Rob. 1
REPERCUSSION UNIT.

CMP Records CMP 31 CS
REPERCUSSION UNIT.

MANNEKE, DAAN (1939-)

-Pneoo II
For winds and percussion.
Attacca Babel 8207-2

MARBE, MYRIAM (1931-)

-Cycle
For flute, guitar and percussion.
Elect ST-ECE 01459
VOICU VASINCA (percussion).

MARKOVITCH, MITCH

-Tornado
SST (Star Sound Tonprod.) 0 164

MAROS, MIKLOS (1943-)

-Dimensions
Caprice CAP 1280
STOCKHOLM PERCUSSION ENSEMBLE.

MAROS, RUDOLF (1917-)

-Four Studies
For 4 percussion players.
Hungaroton SLPX-12368

MARTA, ISTVAN

-Doll's House Story (1985)
Hungaroton HCD 12855 (Compact Disc)
AMADINDA PERCUSSION GROUP.

Hungaroton SLPD 12800
AMADINDA PERCUSSION GROUP.

MARTIRANO, SALVATORE (1927-)

-Underworld
For tenor saxophone, 4 percussionists, 2 double basses, and tape.
Heliodor H-25047

MATHER, BRUCE (1939-)

-Clos de Vougeot (1977)
Nexus NE 05
NEXUS.

MATSUDAIRA, YORI-AKI (1931-)

-Rhymes for Gazzelloni
For flute and percussion.
Wergo WER 60 029

MATSUMOTO, HINOHARU

-Vanishing Point - Archiphase VII
Camerata Tokyo CMT-1086
SUMIRE YOSHIHARA (percussion).

MAULDIN, MICHAEL

-Glyph
For clarinet, vibraphone, and piano.
Opus One 52
ROBYN SCHULKOSKI (vibraphone).

MAXWELL DAVIES, PETER (1934-)

-Eight Songs for a Mad King (1969)
Opus One 26
PETER TANNER (percussion).

-Sonatium
For solo percussion.
L'Oisseau Lyre DSLO-1
STOMU YAMASH'TA (percussion).

-Turris Campanarum Sonatium
L'Oisseau Lyre DSLO-1
STOMU YAMASH'TA (percussion).

MAY, THEODORE

-**Para-Diddle** (1979)
Opus One 80/81
THE PERCUSSION GROUP -
CINCINNATI

MAYS, THEODORE (1941-   )

-**6 Invocations to the Svara Mandala**
CRI S-344
WICHITA STATE UNIVERSITY
PERCUSSION ORCHESTRA. J. C. Combs,
conductor.

MAYUZUMI, TOSHIRO (1929-   )

-**Concerto for Percussion**
AWS KP-101
AMERICAN WIND SYMPHONY
ORCHESTRA.

McKENZIE, JACK H. (1930-   )

-**Introduction and Allegro**
Urania UX-106
AMERICAN PERCUSSION SOCIETY.

-**Nonet**
For bongo drums, small conga or
small tenor drum, large conga or
large tenor drum, gourd, bass drum,
cowbell, tam-tam, suspended cymbal,
maracas, claves, 4 tom-toms, and
marimbula or temple blocks.
Golden Crest CR 4004

-**Rites** (1957)
CRS 6   University of Illinois School
of Music Custom Recording Series.
UNIVERSITY OF ILLINOIS
PERCUSSION ENSEMBLE. Jack
McKenzie, conductor.

-**Three Dances**
Golden Crest CR 4004

McKINLEY, WILLIAM THOMAS (1938-   )

-**Paintings VII** (1982)
For bass clarinet, harp, piano,
violin, viola, cello, and percussion.
CRI SD-507
FRANK EPSTEIN (percussion).

MEDEK, TILO (1940-   )

-**Lerina** (1974)
For marimba.
SCHW 1 026
WOLFGANG PREISSLER (marimba).

-**Reliquienschrein**
For organ and percussion.
SCHW 1 017
CHRISTIAN RODERBURG
(percussion).

-**Unkeler Fahr**
For organ and percussion.
SCHW 1 017
CHRISTIAN RODERBURG
(percussion).

MEIER, JOST (1939-   )

-**Sonata a cinque**
For clarinet, violin, cello, piano, and
percussion.
Gallo 30-239

MEKEEL, JOYCE (1931-   )

-**Rune** (1977)
For flute and percussion.
North NR 203
D. ANDERSON (percussion).

MERCURE, PIERRE

-**Tetrachromie**
For alto sax, clarinet, bass clarinet,
percussion, and magnetic band.
Columbia MS-6763

MERILAINEN, USKO (1930-   )

-**Concerto for Double Bass and
Percussion Instruments** (1973)
Finlandia FA 339
RAINER KUISMA (percussion).

MESSIAEN, OLIVIER (1908-   )

-**Couleurs de la cité céleste**
For 3 clarinets, 4 trumpets, 2 horns,
3 trombones, 1 bass trombone, piano
solo, xylophone, xylorimba,
marimba, tuned cowbells, tubular
bells, 4 gongs, and 2 tam-tams.
Columbia MS-7356
LES PERCUSSIONS DE STRASBOURG.

-Et Exspecto Resurrectionem Mortuorum
For woodwinds, brass, and metallic percussion instruments.
Columbia MS-7356
LES PERCUSSIONS DE STRASBOURG.

-Seven Haikai
Everest 3192
LES PERCUSSIONS DE STRASBOURG.

MHS 3031 W
GERARD PEROTIN (xylophone).

MÉTRAL, PIERRE (1936-)

-Repercussion. (Ballet for 4 percussion instruments) (1965)
Gallo 30-147
GENEVA PERCUSSION ENSEMBLE.

-Sonatina No. 1 (1967)
For violin and percussion.
Gallo 30-147
GENEVA PERCUSSION ENSEMBLE.

MIKI, MINORU (1930-)

-Concerto for Marimba and Orchestra (Excerpts).
Candide/Vox Records CE 31051
KEIKO ABE (marimba).
(Complete Version)
Denon 30C0-1729 (Compact Disc)
KEIKO ABE (marimba).

-Time for Marimba
Denon 30C0-1727 (Compact Disc)
KEIKO ABE (marimba).

Nippon Columbia Co., Ltd OQ-7466
KEIKO ABE (marimba).

Studio 4 Productions S4P-R101
KAREN ERVIN (marimba).

MILHAUD, DARIUS (1892-1974)

-Concerto for Marimba, Vibraphone, and Orchestra (1947)
AUL 53 576
WOLFGANG PACHLA (marimba and vibraphone). With the Nurnmberg Symphony Orchestra. Franz Allers, cond.

BIS LP-149
RAINER KUISMA (marimba and vibraphone). With the Norrköping Symphony Orchestra.

-Concerto for Percussion and Small Orchestra
Candide 31013
FAURE DANIEL (percussion).

FSM 33 1 013
FAURE DANIEL (percussion).

-Création du Monde (1923)
Angel CDC 47845

Charlin SLC-17

Nonesuch 71281

Victrola ALK1-5391

-Second Concerto
For two pianos and percussion.
MHS 854
JEAN-CLAUDE CASADESUS, JEAN-PIERRE DROUET, DIEGO MASON, and JEAN-CHARLES FRANCOIS (percussion).

MILLER, EDWARD (1930-)

-Quartet Variations (1972)
Opus One 22
BLACKEARTH PERCUSSION GROUP.

MILLER, MALLOY (1917-1981)

-Prelude for Percussion (1956)
For glockenspiel, xylophone, tom-tom, snare drum, wood block, two cymbals, whip, tambourine, triangle, bass drum, suspended cymbal, and four timpani.
Orion 642
PRICE PERCUSSION ENSEMBLE.

Period Records SPL 743
MICHAEL COLGRASS, JACK JENNINGS, PHILIP BROWN, SAL BUCCOLA, MEL DVORKEN, and WARREN SMITH (percussion).

MIYOSHI, AKIRA (1933-   )

-**Concerto pour Marimba et Ensemblé a Cordes**
Candide/Vox Records CE 31051
KEIKO ABE (marimba).

Denon 30C0-1728 (Compact Disc)
KEIKO ABE (marimba).

-**Conversation**
For marimba.
Candide/Vox Records CE 31051
KEIKO ABE (marimba).

Denon 30C0-1727 (Compact Disc)
KEIKO ABE (marimba).

Nippon Columbia Co., Ltd.   OQ-7466
KEIKO ABE (marimba).

-**Nocturne**
For five players.
Denon 38C37-7280 (Compact Disc)
KEIKO ABE (marimba); MAKOTO
ARUGA (percussion) (THE TOKYO
QUINTET).

-**Torse III** (1968)
For marimba.
AUD 63 407
AXEL FRIES (marimba).

Candide/Vox Records CE 31051
KEIKO ABE (marimba).

Denon 30C0-1727 (Compact Disc)
KEIKO ABE (marimba).

Nippon Columbia Co., Ltd.   OQ-7466
KEIKO ABE (marimba).

MIZELLE, DARY JOHN

-**Polytempus II** (1980)
For marimba and computer
generated tape.
Lumina L 002
OBERLIN PERCUSSION GROUP.

-**Soundscape** (1976)
Lumina L 002
OBERLIN PERCUSSION GROUP.

MOEUS, ROBERT (1920-   )

-**A Brief Mass**
For choir, organ, vibraphone,
guitar, and double bass.
CRI SD-262

-**Concerto Grosso** (1968)
For piano, percussion, and
orchestra.
CRI S-457
RAYMOND DesROCHES, RICHARD FITZ,
LOUIS ODDO, BRUCE PATTI, and
STEPHEN PAYSON (percussion).

MOISY, HEINZ von (1935-   )

-**Praca Maua**
For percussion.
SST 0 164
PERCUSSION ENSEMBLE OF THE
BADISCHEN CONSERVATORY.
THO MTH 124
PERCUSSION ENSEMBLE SIEGFRIED
FINK.

MONTGOMERY, JAMES

-**Chaser** (1978)
For two horns, tape, random voltage
generator, and percussion.
Music Gallery Editions MGE 21

MONTI, VITTORIO (1868-1922)

-**Csárdás** (arr. T. Sasaki)
MHS 4856Y
TATSUO SASAKI (xylophone).

MORI, KRODO

-**Tenebroso Giorno**
For percussion.
CBS Sony 32DC-1009 (Compact Disc)
SUMIRE YOSHIHARA (percussion).

MOSKO, LUCKY   See: **BERGAMO, JOHN**

MOSKO, STEPHEN

-**The Cosmology of Easy Listening**
(1978)
Opus One 80/81
THE PERCUSSION GROUP -
CINCINNATI.

MOSS, DAVID (1949-)

-Niche
CPR 007
DAVID MOSS (percussion).

-Phrase.
CPR 007
DAVID MOSS (percussion).

-Talk.
CPR 007
DAVID MOSS (percussion).

-Terrain 1-7.
CPR 007
DAVID MOSS (percussion).

-Tongue.
CPR 007
DAVID MOSS (percussion).

MOSS, LAWRENCE (1927-)

-Toot Sweet
For oboe and percussion.
Opus One 31
ALBERT MERZ and DONALD BICK
(percussion).

MOSKOWSKI, MORITZ (1854-1925)

-Bolero (arr. G. H. Green)
Conservatory 7101 M
GEORGE HAMILTON GREEN
(xylophone).

MOSZUMANSKA-NAZAR, KRYSTYNA (1924-)

-Interpretations
For flute, percussion, and magnetic
tape.
MUZA M-3 XW-1034
J. STEFANSKI (percussion).

MOZART, WOLFGANG AMADEUS (1756-1791)

-Divertimento No.1 in D Major, K.136
For four marimbas.
Firebird K33Y 200 (Compact Disc)
TOKYO MARIMBA ENSEMBLE. Makoto
Aruga, conductor.

-Divertimento No.17 in D Major, K.334
For four marimbas and two horns.
Firebird K33Y 200 (Compact Disc)
TOKYO MARIMBA ENSEMBLE. Makoto
Aruga, conductor.

MUMMA, GORDON (1935-)

-Peasant Boy
For piano, bass, drums, and magnetic
tape.
ESP-Disk 1009

MUSSER, CLAIR OMAR

-Etude Op. 6 No. 2 in A-flat Major
Epic P-17808
VIDA CHENOWETH (marimba).

Studio 4 Productions S4P R-100
GORDON STOUT (marimba).

-Etude Op. 6 No. 8 ("Whole-Tone Etude" - 1948)
For marimba.
Studio 4 Productions S4P R-101
KAREN ERVIN (marimba).

-Etude Op. 6 No. 9 in B Major
For marimba.
Epic P-17808
VIDA CHENOWETH (marimba).

-Etude Op. 6 No. 10 in C Major (1948)
For marimba.
AUD 63 407
AXEL FRIES (marimba).

Epic P-17808
VIDA CHENOWETH (marimba).

Studio 4 Productions S4P R-101
KAREN ERVIN (marimba).

-Prelude Op. 11 No. 3 in G Major
Epic P-17808
VIDA CHENOWETH (marimba).

Studio 4 Productions S4P R-100
GORDON STOUT (marimba).

N

NAKADA, YOSHINAO (1923-   )

-The Snow-Clad Town
For marimba and recorder.
Denon OF-7163-ND
KEIKO ABE (marimba) and WALTER
VAN HAUWE (recorder).

Denon 33C37-7393 (Compact Disc)
KEIKO ABE (marimba) and WALTER
VAN HAUWE (recorder).

NARITA, TAMEZO

-Song of the Seashore
For marimba and recorder.
Denon OF-7163-ND
KEIKO ABE (marimba) and WALTER
VAN HAUWE (recorder).

Denon 33C37-7393 (Compact Disc)
KEIKO ABE (marimba) and WALTER
VAN HAUWE (recorder).

NAUMANN, SIEGFRIED (1919-   )

-Bombarda, Op. 27 (1973)
For organ and percussion.
Cap 1 175
BJORN LILJEQUIST (percussion).

NEIL, AL

-Lombardo
For piano, voice, zither, tinfoil,
percussion, bass, soprano sax, and
tape recorder.
SEE (See/Hear Productions-Canada)
ST-55852
GREGG SIMPSON (percussion).

NEVIN, ETHELBERT (1862-1901)

-Mighty Lak'A Rose (arr. B. Becker)
Nexus NE 01
BOB BECKER (marimba).

NEWELL, ROBERT

-Spirals
For tenor, mezzo-soprano, and
percussion.
Advance 25-S
JOE KUCERA (percussion).

NEXUS (PERCUSSION ENSEMBLE)   See
also: CAHN, WILLIAM; NEVIN,
ETHELBERT,
and SILVERS/De SYLVA

-Amazing Space
Nexus NE-01
NEXUS.

-An African Song
Nexus NE-01
NEXUS.

-Kobina
Nexus NE-01
NEXUS.

-Passage
Nexus NE-01
NEXUS.

-Unexpected Pleasures
Nexus NE-01
NEXUS.

NIEWIADOMSKA, BARBARA

-Tinta e Ritmo
MUZA SXL 0809

NIKURA, KEN (1951-   )

-Gong Ekasama Budaya (1979)
For clarinet, piano, and percussion.
Japan Federation of Composers JFC-
R8702; Fontec FO-2517
TOSHIYUKI MATSUKURA
(percussion).

NILOVIC, JANKO (1941-   )

-Suite Balkanique
For trombones and percussion.
Crystal 223

NILSSON, BO (1937-)

-Bass (1977)
For tuba and percussion.
Cap 1 143
BJORN LILJEQUIST (percussion).

NODA, TERUYUKI (1940-)

-Eclogue (1976)
For flute and percussion.
Camerata Tokyo CMT-1059
SUMIRE YOSHIHARA (percussion).

RCA Japan RDC 1

-Obsession
For marimba, flute, clarinet,
contrabass, and percussion.
Denon 38C37-7280 (Compact Disc)
KEIKO ABE (marimba), MAKOTO
ARUGA (percussion) (THE TOKYO
QUINTET).

**-Quinteto per marimba, 3 flauti, e
contrabasso "Mattinata"**
Candide/Vox Records CE 31051
KEIKO ABE (marimba).

Denon Japan C37-7294
KEIKO ABE (marimba).

Denon 30C0-1728 (Compact Disc)
KEIKO ABE (marimba).

NORDHEIM, ARNE

-Response I
For 2 percussion groups and tape.
Limelight-LS 86 061
PER NYHAUG and PER ERIK THORSEN
(percussion).

Phillips 839250-AY

Phillips France - 836.896 DSY

NORGÅRD, PER (1932-)

-I Ching
For percussion instruments.
BIS LP-256
GERT MORTENSEN (percussion).

-Rondo
Cambridge 2824
THE COPENHAGEN PERCUSSION
ENSEMBLE.

-Waves
Cambridge 2824
THE COPENHAGEN PERCUSSION
ENSEMBLE.

Camerata Tokyo CMT-1040
SUMIRE YOSHIHARA (percussion).

NORVO, RED

-Dance of the Octopus
Mercury (Golden Imports) SRI 75108
THE EASTMAN MARIMBA BAND.

NOWAK, LIONEL

-Concert Piece for Kettledrums
CRI S-260
LOUIS CALABRO (kettledrums).

NUOVA CONSONANZA GRUPPE

-Credo
For double bass, percussion, and
piano.
DGG 137007
EGISTO MACCHI (percussion).

DGG 643541

RCA MILDS 20273

-Epoi
For percussion, double bass, cello,
trombone, piano, and trumpet.
DGG 137007
MARIO BERTONCINI and EGISTO
MACCHI (percussion).

RCA MILDS 20273

-Improvisationen
For percussion, double bass, cello,
trombone, piano, and trumpet.
DGG 643541
MARIO BERTONCINI and EGISTO
MACCHI (percussion).

O

OAK, KIL-SUNG (1945-   )

-Amorphosis (1971)
For soprano, glockenspiel, marimba,
vibraphone, xylophone, celesta,
chimes, timpani, side drum, snare
drum, suspended cymbal, sizzle
cymbal, tam-tam, gong, slapstick,
and temple blocks.
Nonesuch H-71291
NEW JERSEY PERCUSSION ENSEMBLE.
Raymond DesRoches, conductor.

O'BRIEN, EUGENE (1945-   )

-Allures (1979)
CRI SD-466
THE PERCUSSION GROUP -
CINCINNATI.

O'DONNELL, RICH (1937-   ) See:
HAMILTON, TOM

OHANA, MAURICE (1914-   )

**-Etude d'interprétation No. 11 and
No.12**
For piano and percussion.
Auvidis AV 4831
GORDON GOTTLIEB (percussion).

-Etudes choreographiques
Caprice CAP 1280
STOCKHOLM PERCUSSION ENSEMBLE.

-4 Etudes choreographiques
Phillips 836.990 DSY
LES PERCUSSIONS DE STRASBOURG.

Phillips Stereo 6718.040
LES PERCUSSIONS DE STRASBOURG.

OKASAKA, KEIKI (1940-   )

-Transition
For percussion ensemble.
Fontec RFO-1040
TOMOYUKI OKADA PERCUSSION
ENSEMBLE.

OLIVEROS, PAULINE (1932-   )

-Outline (An Improvisation Chart)
For flute, percussion, and string
bass.
Nonesuch H-71237
RONALD GEORGE (percussion).

ORTIZ-ALVARADO, WILLIAM

-124 East 107th Street (1979)
For percussion.
Opus One 99
UNIVERSITY OF BUFFALO
PERCUSSION ENSEMBLE.

ORTON, RICHARD

-Cycle
Mainstream 5001
RICHARD ORTON (percussion).

OTTE, HANS (1926-   )

-Alpha-Omega II (1965)
For 12 male voices, organ, and
percussion.
Wergo WER 60 026
ERICH SEILER and KARLHEINZ
BENDER (percussion).

**-Daidalos - Ballet in 7 Scenes for 6
Players (Scene 3)**
HM DMR 1010/12
CHRISTOPH CASKEL and SIEGFRIED
ROCKSTROH (percussion).

OWEN, CHARLES (1912-1985)

-Lover (1972)
University of Michigan SM-0016
UNIVERSITY OF MICHIGAN
PERCUSSION ENSEMBLE. Charles
Owen, director.

P

PACHELBEL, JOHANN (1653-1706)

Kanon in D Major
CBS Records M-39704 Stereo
BRIAN SLAWSON (keyboard
percussion).

CBS MK-39704 (Compact Disc)
BRIAN SLAWSON (keyboard
percussion).

For percussion ensemble   (arr. **H.
Farberman**
MMG 115 (D)
THE ALL STAR PERCUSSION ENSEMBLE.

MMG MCD 10007 (Compact Disc)
THE ALL STAR PERCUSSION ENSEMBLE.

PACHLA, WOLFGANG (1913-1982)

-**Etudes for Marimba**

a-moll	Es-dur
b-moll	F-dur
c-moll	fis-moll
cis-moll	G-dur
E-dur	gis-moll
e-moll	h-moll

AUL 53 576
WOLFGANG PACHLA (marimba).

PAGANINI, NICCOLO (1782-1840)

-**Sonata Concertata**
For marimba and cello.
Golden Crest 4223 (D)
STEVEN BROWN (percussion).

PANUFNIK, ANDRZEJ (1914-   )

-**Concertino** (1980)
For timpani, percussion , and
strings.
Unicorn-Kanchana Digital DKP 9016
KURT-HANS GOEDICKE (timpani) and
MICHAEL FRYE (percussion).

-**Metasinfonia**
For organ, strings, and timpani.
Unicorn Kanchana Digital DKP 9049
KURT-HANS GOEDICKE (timpani).

PAROLARI, RETO (1952-   )

-**Csardas fabol**
For marimba and piano.
SP 10 019
RETO PAROLARI (percussion).

-**Spanische Skisse G-dur** (1980/83)
For oboe, marimba, and piano.
SP 10 019
RETO PAROLARI (marimba).

PARRAN, J.D. See: HAMILTON, TOM

PARRIS, ROBERT (1924-   )

-**Book of Imaginary Beings, The**
For flute, violin, cello, piano, celeste,
and percussion.
Turnabout 34568

-**Concerto**
For percussion, violin, cello, and
pianoforte.
Orion 78301
RONALD BARNETT (percussion).

PARTCH, HARRY (1901-1974)

-**And On the Seventh Day, Petals Fell
in Petaluma**
CRI ACS-6001

CRI S-213
GATE 5 ENSEMBLE.

-**The Bewitched** (1957) (Complete)
2 CRI SD-304
UNIVERSITY OF ILLINOIS ENSEMBLE.

-**The Bewitched: Final Scene and
Epilogue**
CRI ACS-6001
GATE 5 ENSEMBLE.

CRI SD-193

-**Castor and Pollux** (from **Plectra
and Percussion Dances**) (1953)
CRI ACS-6001
GATE 5 ENSEMBLE.

CRI SD-193

-**Cloud Chamber Music** (1950)
CRI ACS-6001
GATE 5 ENSEMBLE.

CRI SD-193

-**The Letter** (1943)
CRI ACS-6001
GATE 5 ENSEMBLE.

CRI SD-193

-**Delusion of the Fury**
2 CBS M2-30576

-**Windsong** (Film Score) (1958)
CRI SD-193
GATE 5 ENSEMBLE.

PARTOS, OEDOEN (1907-1977)

-**Agada**
For viola, piano, and percussion.
CBS S-72821
JOEL THOME (percussion).

PATACHICH, IVAN (1922-)

-**Antiphons** (1977)
For violin, percussion, and tape.
Hungaroton SLPX 12369
ZOLTAN RACZ (percussion).

-**Metamorphosi** (1978)
For marimba and tape recorder.
Hungaroton SLPX 12065
GABOR KOSA (percussion).

PECK, RUSSELL (1925-)

-**Automobile**
For soprano, flute, percussion, and
double bass.
CRI S-367
DAVID JOHNSON (percussion).

-**Lift Off** (1966/75)
Opus One 80/81
THE PERCUSSION GROUP -
CINCINNATI.

PELLMAN, SAMUEL (1953-)

-**Crane Songs**
For soprano, flute, clarinet, violin,
piano, and percussion.
Redwood ES-24

PELUSI, MARIO

-**Concert Piece**
For baritone saxophone, brass
quartet, and percussion.
Crystal S-152

• **PENDERECKI, KRZYSZTOF (1933-)**

-**Anaklasis** (1960)
For strings and percussion.
EMI 065-102 452-1

Wergo WER 60 020

-**Psalmen Davids** (1958)
For choir and percussion.
Cantate CAN 658 225
PERCUSSION ENSEMBLE SIEGFRIED
FINK.

Wergo WER 60 020

PENN, WILLIAM (1943-)

-**Four Preludes for Leigh Howard
Stevens**
For marimba.
CRI S-367
LEIGH HOWARD STEVENS (marimba).

PENHERSKI, ZBIGNIEW

-**Incantationi**
MUZA SX 2092
WARSAW PERCUSSION GROUP.

PERRY, JULIA (1924-1979)

-**Homunculus C.F.** (1960)
For ten percussionists.
CRI S-252
MANHATTAN PERCUSSION ENSEMBLE.
Paul Price, conductor.

PETERS, MITCHELL

-**Yellow After the Rain**
For marimba.
Studio 4 Productions S4P R-102
GORDON STOUT (marimba).

PFISTER, HUGO (1914-1969)

-**Agaisches Tagebuch**
For oboe, strings, and percussion.
FSM 0 530
DIETER DYK (percussion).

PICHÉ, JEAN (1951-)

-**Steal the Thunder**
For percussion.
Centredisques (Canada) WRC1-4951
BEVERLEY JOHNSTON (percussion).

PILLIN, BORIS (1940-)

-**Concerto for Strings and Percussion**
(1981)
WIM 22

-**Duo** (1971)
For percussion and piano.
WIM 5
KAREN ERVIN (percussion).

-**Tune in C** (1975)
For piano and percussion.
WIM 11
BARRY SILVERMAN (percussion).

POPPER, DAVID (1843-1913)

-**Hungarian Rhapsody, Op. 68** (arr. T. Sasaki)
MHS 4856Y
TATSUO SASAKI (xylophone).

PORCELIJN, DAVID (1947-   )

-**Requiem for Percussion** (1970)
DAVS 7273/3
PERCUSSION GROUP AMSTERDAM.

-**10-5-6-5 (a)**
For 2 string quartets, wind quintet and
2 vibraphones.
DAVS 7273/4

POULENC, FRANCIS (1899-1963)

-**Sonata** (From **Sonata for flute and piano**) (arr. T. Sasaki)
MHS 4856Y
TATSUO SASAKI (xylophone).

POWELL, MORGAN (1938-   )

-**Duet V**
TR² 001
MICHAEL UDOW (percussion)
with THE TONE ROAD RAMBLERS.

-**Fine Tuning**
TR² 001
MICHAEL UDOW (percussion)
with THE TONE ROAD RAMBLERS.

PRIN, JEAN BAPTISTE (? - 1742)

-**L'echo de Psyche**
For timpani, trumpet, and organ.
Schwann Musica Mundi CD 11066
WERNER THÄRICHEN or NICHOLAS
BARDACH (timpani).

PROKOFIEV, SERGEI (1891-1953)

-**Field of the Dead** (arr. R. Gipson)
For percussion ensemble.
Second Hearing GS 9008
UNIVERSITY OF OKLAHOMA
PERCUSSION ENSEMBLE.

PTASZYNSKA, MARTA (1943-   )

-**Space Model** (1975)
For one percussionist.
Pro Viva/Die Neue
Schallplattenlabel fur Neue Musik.
Best. Nv. ISPV-1987
(Munich, West Germany)
MARTA PTASZYNSKA (percussion).

-**Epigrams** (1977)
For women voices, flute, piano, harp, and   percussion.
Pro Viva/Die Neue
Schallplattenlabel fur Neue Musik.
Best. Nv. ISPV-1987
(Munich, West Germany)
MARTA PTASZYNSKA (percussion).

-**Jeu-Parti** (1980)
For vibraphone and harp.
Polskie Nagrania. MUZA SX (Warsaw, Poland)
HUBERT RUTKOWSKI (vibraphone).

PUIG, MICHAEL

-**Provisoires Agglomerats**
For speaker, female voice, choir, magnetic band, and percussion.
Philips France 836.992 DSY
LES PERCUSSIONS DE STRASBOURG.

PUSZTAI, TIBOR (1946-   )

-**Interactions** (1976)
For horn and percussion.
Crystal S-673
INDIANA PERCUSSION ENSEMBLE.
George Gaber, director.

R

RAPHLING, SAM (1910-   )

-**Concerto for piano and percussion**
Serenus 12061
LONDON PERCUSSION ENSEMBLE.

RAKACH, ENRIQUE (1932-)

-Imaginary Landscape
For flute and percussion.
Composers' Voice (DAVS) 7475/2
WILLY GOUDSWAARD (percussion).

REA, JOHN (1944-)

-Reception and Offering Music
For winds and percussion.
Melbourne SMLP 4040
RUSSELL HARTENBERGER
(percussion).

READ, GARDNER (1913-)

-The Aztec Gods (Los Dioses Aztecas)
For percussion.
CRI S-444
PAUL PRICE PERCUSSION ENSEMBLE.

REGNER, HERMANN (1928-)

-Changing Patterns
For eight congas.
Wergo WER 60123
JURGEN FRIEDEL, STEFAN
GAGELMANN, MATTHIAS JAKOB, AND
ELMAR KOLB (congas).

Wergo WER 60123-50 (Compact Disc)
JURGEN FRIEDEL, STEFAN
GAGELMANN, MATTHIAS JAKOB, AND
ELMAR KOLB (congas).

REICH, STEVE (1936-)

-Clapping Music (1972)
Elektra Nonesuch 9 79169-1
STEVE REICH and RUSS
HARTENBERGER (hand clapping).

-Drumming
For small tuned drums, marimbas,
voices, glockenspiels, whistling, and
piccolo.
3 DG 2740106
RUSS HARTENBERGER, BOB BECKER,
JAMES PREISS, STEVE REICH, TIM
FERCHEN, STEVE CHAMBERS,
CORNELIUS CARDEW, BEN HARMS, and
GLEN VELEZ (small tuned drums,
marimbas, and glockenspiels).

Elektra Nonesuch Digital 9 79170-1
STEVE REICH AND MUSICIANS.

-Four Organs
For four electric organs and maracas.
Angel S-36059
TOM RANEY (maracas)

Shandar SR 10.005
JON GIBSON(maracas).

-Music for a Large Ensemble
ECM/Warner Brothers 1168

-Music for 18 Musicians
ECM/Warner Brothers 1129

-Music for Mallet Instruments,
Voices, and Organ (1973)
DG 2535463
REICH ENSEMBLE.

3 DG 2740106
RUSS HARTENBERGER, BOB BECKER,
TIM FERCHEN, and STEVE REICH
(marimbas); GLEN VELEZ and BEN
HARMS (glockenspiels), and JAMES
PREISS (metallophone).

-Music for Pieces of Wood (1973)
Hungaroton SLPX 12545
GROUP 180

Nexus NE 05
NEXUS.

-Piano Phase (1967)
Camerata Tokyo CMT-1059
YASUNORI YAMAGUCHI and SUMIRE
YOSHIHARA (marimbas).

Elektra Nonesuch 9 79169-1
REICH ENSEMBLE.
Hungaroton HCD 12855 (Compact Disc)
AMADINDA PERCUSSION GROUP.

Hungaroton SLPD 12800
AMADINDA PERCUSSION GROUP.

-Sextet (1985)
For marimba, vibraphone, bass drum,
crotales, tam-tam, sticks, and
synthesizer.
Nonesuch 79138-1
BOB BECKER, RUSS HARTENBERGER,
GARY KVISTAD, and GLEN VELEZ
(percussion).

Nonesuch 9 79138-2 (Compact Disc)
BOB BECKER, RUSS HARTENBERGER,
GARY KVISTAD, and GLEN VELEZ
(percussion).

-Six Marimbas (1973/86)
For six marimbas.
Nonesuch   79138-1
BOB BECKER, RUSS HARTENBERGER,
KORY GROSSMAN, JAMES PREISS, BILL
RUYLE, and WILLIAM TRIGG
(marimbas).

Nonesuch 9 79138-2 (Compact Disc)
BOB BECKER, RUSS HARTENBERGER,
KORY GROSSMAN, JAMES PREISS, BILL
RUYLE, and WILLIAM TRIGG
(marimbas).

-Six Pianos
DG 2535463
REICH ENSEMBLE.

3 DG 2740106
STEVE CHAMBERS, JAMES PREISS,
RUSS HARTENBERGER, BOB BECKER,
STEVE REICH, and GLEN VELEZ
(pianos).

REYNOLDS, ROGER (1934-   )

-From Behind the Unreasoning Mask
For trombone and percussion.
NW 237
TOM RANEY and ROGER REYNOLDS
(percussion).

-Ping (1968)
For piano, flute, harmonioum,
percussion, and electric sounds.
CRI SD-285
PAUL CHIHARA (percussion).

-"...the serpent-snapping eye."
(1978)
For piano, percussion, trumpet, and
tape.
CRI SD-495
PRATT (percussion).

RIEDL, JOSEF ANTON

-Komposition fuer Konkrete und
electronische Klaenge
DGG 654 062
MICHAEL LEWIS and MICHAEL
RANTA (percussion).

-Live Nr. 4 III
DGG 654 062
MICHAEL LEWIS and MICHAEL
RANTA (percussion).

-Tonbaender und fuer verschiedene
instrumente und Stimmen
DGG 654 062
MICHAEL LEWIS and MICHAEL
RANTA (percussion).

RILEY, TERRY (1935-   )

-In C
Columbia Stereo MS-7178
EDWARD BURNHAM (vibes) and JAN
WILLIAMS (marimbaphone).

ROCCISANO, JOSEPH (1939-   )

-Sonorities
For saxophone, cello, and percussion.
Protone 153

RODBY JOHN (1944-   )

-Septet (1974-75)
For strings, sax, oud, piano, and
percussion.
Crystal S-505

RODRIGUE, NICOLE (1943-   )

-Fission
For two percussionists.
CAPAC QC-1274

-Modules
For harp, contrabass, and seven tam-
tams.
CAPAC QC-1274

-Nasca
For clarinet, alto piano, and
vibraphone.
CAPAC QC-1274

ROLDAN, AMADEO (1900-1939)

-Two Ritmicas (1930)
For claves, quijada, cencerro, guiro,
maracas, bongos, timbales Cubanos,
timbales de orquesta, bombo, and
marimba.
Mainstream Records MS/5011
ZITA CARNO, GERALD JACOBOSKY,
RICHARD ALLEN, MICHAEL
ROSENBERG, SAL BUCOLA, DON
DesROCHES, RAY DesROCHES, EDWARD
CORNELIUS, WARREN SMITH, DAMON
BUCKLEY, and GEORGE BOBERG
(percussion).

ROLNICK, NEIL B (1947-   )

-Ever-livin' Rhythm
For percussion and tape.
1750 Arch 1793
GORDON GOTTLIEB (percussion).

ROREM, NED (1923-   )

-Lovers
For harpsichord, oboe, cello, and
percussion.
Serenus 12056

ROSALES (arr. Musser)

-Bolero
Mark Records MES 38080
THE 1978 P.A.S.I.C. MARIMBA
ORCHESTRA.

ROSELL, LARS-ERIK (1944-   )

-Poem in the Dark
For mezzo, flutes, trombone, double
bass, and percussion.
BIS 32

ROSENMAN, LEONARD (1924-   )

-Chamber Music V (1979)
For flute, clarinet, viola, cello, piano,
and percussion.
CRI S-486
FRANK EPSTEIN and THOMAS GAUGER

ROUSE, CHRISTOPHER (1949-   )

-Infernal Machine, The (1981)
For orchestra.
Nonesuch Digital 79118
SAINT LOUIS SYMPHONY ORCHESTRA.

-Ku-Ka-Ilimoku (1978)
University of Michigan SM-0016
UNIVERSITY OF MICHIGAN
PERCUSSION ENSEMBLE. Charles
Owen, director.

-Ogoun Badagris (1976)
For percussion quintet.
Nonesuch Digital 79118
RICHARD HOLMES, JOHN KASICA,
RICHARD O'DONNELL, THOMAS
STUBBS, and ALAN SCHILLING
(percussion).

RUDZINSKI, ZBIGNIEW

-Campanella
For percussion group.
MUZA SX 1595
THE PERCUSSION GROUP IN POZNAN.
Zbigniew Rudzinski, conductor.

-Trytony/The Tryton
MUZA SX 2092
WARSAW PERCUSSION GROUP.

RUSSELL, ARMAND

-Percussion Suite
For three percussionists.
Trio PA-4010
TOMOYUKI OKADA, MITSUAKI
IMAMURA, and KAZUKI MOMOSE
(percussion).

RUSSELL, WILLIAM (1905-   )

-Three Cuban Pieces (1939)
For cencerros, maracas, guiro, claves,
quijada, marimbula, and bongo
drums.
Mainstream Records MS/5011
EDWARD CORNELIUS, PAUL PRICE,
GEORGE BOBERG, and RAY DesROCHES
(percussion).

-**Three Dance Movements** (1933)
For small triangle, dinner bell, large triangle, bottle, anvil, tom-toms, finger cymbal, suspended Turkish cymbal, suspended Chinese cymbal, pair of cymbals, small wood block, snare drum, large wood block, bass drum, piano, and slapstick.
Mainstream Records MS/5011
PAUL PRICE, GEORGE BOBERG, RAY DesROCHES, and ZITA CARNO (percussion).

RUSSO, JOHN (1943-   )

-**Four Riffs**
For clarinet and percussion.
CBS 8219
GLEN STEELE (percussion).

-**Sonata No. 5**
For clarinet, piano, and percussion.
Orion 78294
FLORENCE LERARDI and ANDREW POWER (percussion).

RZEWSKI, FREDERIC (1938-   )

-**Attica** (1972)
For speaker, vibraphone, piccolo trumpet, alto sax, viola, trombone, piano, and bass.
Hungaroton SLPX 12545
GROUP 180

Opus One 20
KARL BERGER (vibraphone).

-**Coming Together** (1972)
For speaker, vibraphone, synthesizer, alto sax, viola, trombone, piano, electric piano, and bass.
Hungaroton SLPX 12545
GROUP 180

Opus One 20
KARL BERGER (vibraphone).

-**Les Moutons de Panurge** (1969)
For vibraphone, glockenspiel, almglocken, nabimba, and xylophone.
Opus One 20
BLACKEARTH PERCUSSION GROUP.

-**Song and Dance** (1977)
For flute, clarinet, bass clarinet, contrabass, and vibraphone.
Nonesuch H-71366

S

SAINT-SAENS, CAMILE (1835-1921)

-**Adagio** (From the Organ Symphony). For percussion ensemble. (arr. R. Gipson)
Second Hearing GS 9008
UNIVERSITY OF OKLAHOMA PERCUSSION ENSEMBLE.

-**Second Concerto in G minor** (trans. Clair Omar Musser)
Mark Records MES 38080
THE 1978 P.A.S.I.C. MARIMBA ORCHESTRA.

SAMKOPF, KJELL (1952-   )

-**Because of G.H** (1981)
Simax PN 2009

-**Intention** (1981)
For marimba, synthesizer, and bells.
Simax PN 2009
KJELL SAMKOPF (marimba).

-**Invention No. 5.** (1981)
For percussion and electronics.
Simax PN 2009
KJELL SAMKOPF (marimba).

-**On the Way.** (1981)
For solo vibraphone.
Simax PN 2009
KJELL SAMKOPF (vibraphone).

SAMUEL, GERHARD (1924-   )

-**What of My Music!** (1979)
For lyric soprano, two solo double basses, 28 tutti basses, and 3 percussionists.
CRI S-422
ALLEN OTTE, JAMES CULEY, and MICHAEL HAKES (percussion).

SAMUELS, DAVE   See also: FRIEDMAN, DAVID

-Sunset Glow
For marimba and vibraphone.
Marimba Productions MP-002
DOUBLE IMAGE (DAVID FRIEDMAN
and DAVE SAMUELS
(marimba/vibraphone).

SANDSTROM, SVEN-DAVID (1942-)

-Drums (1980)
For percussion ensemble.
BIS LP-272
KROUMATA PERCUSSION ENSEMBLE.

BIS CD-272 (Compact Disc)
KROUMATA PERCUSSION ENSEMBLE.

SAPERSTEIN, DAVID (1948-)

-Antiphonies for Percussion (1972)
For 2 bass drums, 4 tenor drums, 2
snare drums, 2 timbales, 4 bongos, 4
gongs, 2 woodblocks, 8 temple
blocks, 4 cowbells, glock, marimba,
vibraphone, xylophone, chimes, 3
suspended cymbals, and 2 antique
cymbals.
Nonesuch H-71291
NEW JERSEY PERCUSSION ENSEMBLE.
Raymond DesRoches, director.

Elektra/Nonesuch 9 79150-2
(Compact Disc)
NEW JERSEY PERCUSSION ENSEMBLE.
Raymond DesRoches, director.

SAPIEYEUSKI, JERZY (1945-)

-Concerto for Viola, Wind Quintet, and Percussion
Crystal S-647
BOATMAN (percussion).

SARMIENTOS, JORGE ALVARO

-Concertino
For marimba and orchestra.
Classic Performances #1 CMP-VC1
VIDA CHENOWETH (marimba). With
the Tulsa Philharmonic. Franco
Autori, cond.

SARY, LASZLO (1940-)

-Pebble Playing in a Pot (1978)
Hungaroton HCD 12855 (Compact
Disc)
AMADINDA PERCUSSION GROUP.

Hungaroton SLPD 12800
AMADINDA PERCUSSION GROUP.

-Sonanti No. 2 (1970).
For flute and percussion.
Hungaroton SLPX 12065
GABOR KOSA (percussion).

SATUREN, DAVID (1939-)

-Trio (1977)
For clarinet, piano, and percussion.
Orion 78294

SCARLATTI, DOMENICO (1685-1757)

-Sonate G-dur
For marimba and vibraphone.
Thorofon MTH 149
PERCUSSION ENSEMBLE SIEGFRIED
FINK.

-Three Sonatas (Longo 404, Longo 82, and Longo 428) (trans. Karen Ervin)
For marimba.
Studio 4 Productions S4P-R101
KAREN ERVIN (marimba).

SCHAT, PETER (1935-)

-Signalement
Phillips 836.991 DSY
LES PERCUSSIONS DE STRASBOURG.

SCHERCHEN-HSIAO, TONA (1938-)

-Shen
For percussion ensemble.
Philips 6521 030
LES PERCUSSIONS DE STRASBOURG.

-Yi pour Marimbaphone
For two marimbists.
Apost AS 37334
KIEFFER and ASKILL (marimba).

SCHMIDT, WILLIAM (1926-   )

-**Jazz Suite**
For 2 tenor saxes and percussion.
WIM 18
BARRY SILVERMAN (percussion).

-**Ludus Americanus** (1971)
For percussion and narrator.
WIM 5
KAREN ERVIN (percussion).

-**Septigrams**
For flute, piano, and percussion.
WIM 2
E. REMSEN (percussion).

SCHOBER, BRIAN

-**Nocturnals**
For piano and percussion.
Auvidis AV 4831
GORDON GOTTLIEB (percussion).

SCHULE, BERNARD

-**Geometrie Animee.**
Pour harpe pre-enregistree,
percussion, et bande magnetique.
CTS 44
STUFF COMBE (percussion).

SCHULLER, GUNTHER (1925-   )

-**Symbiosis** (1957)
For violin, piano, and percussion.
Golden Crest 2007

-**Symphony for Brass and Percussion**
Argo ZRG-731

SCHUYT, NICO (1922-   )

-**Discorsi Capricciosi**
For 12 winds and percussion.
Donemus Audio Visual Series 7002

SEEGER, RUTH CRAWFORD (1901-1953)

-**Three Songs**
For mezzo-soprano, oboe, piano, and
percussion.
CRI SD-501

SERMILA, JARMO

-**Monody** (1975)
For horn and percussion.
Music Gallery Editions MGE 21

SEROCKI, KAZIMIERZ (1922-   )

-**Continuum** (1965-66)
MUZA SX 2092
WARSAW PERCUSSION GROUP.

Philips Stereo 6718 040
LES PERCUSSIONS DE STRASBOURG.

SHAPEY, RALPH (1921-   )

-**Evocation** (1959)
For violin, piano, and percussion.
CRI SD-141

-**Three for Six**
For flute, clarinet, percussion,
piano, violin, and cello.
CRI SD-509
NEW YORK MUSIC ENSEMBLE.

SHIBATA, MINAO (1916-   )

-**Imagery**
For marimba.
Denon 35C37-7279 (Compact Disc)
KEIKO ABE (marimba).

Denon 30C0-1729 (Compact Disc)
KEIKO ABE (marimba).

-**Quadrill**
For marimba.
CBS Sony 32 DC 5027 (Compact Disc)
MICHIKO TAKAHASHI (marimba).

SHIDA, SHOKO (1942-   )

-**MU U**
Asian Sound Records ASR1001
MICHAEL RANTA (percussion).

-**MU UI**
Asian Sound Records ASR1001
MICHAEL RANTA (percussion).

SHIMOYAMA, HIFUMI (1930-   )

-Kyoboku II
For marimba.
CBS Sony 32 DC 5027 (Compact Disc)
MICHIKO TAKAHASHI (marimba)

SHINOHARA, MAKOTO (1931-   )

-Alternances
Philips Stereo 836.991 DSY
LES PERCUSSIONS DE STRASBOURG.

SHOSTAKOVITCH, DIMITRI (1906-1975)

-Polka from The Golden Age (arr.
Anatol Lybimov)
BIS LP-149
RAINER KUISMA (marimba).

-Prelude and Fugue XV
Mark Records MES 38080
THE 1978 P.A.S.I.C. MARIMBA
ORCHESTRA.

-Zwischenspiel Nr. 14 aus "DIE NASE
Thorofon CTH 2003 (Compact Disc)
WURZBURGER PERKUSSIONS
ENSEMBLE.   Siegfried Fink, director.

THO MTH 149
PERCUSSION ENSEMBLE SIEGFRIED
FINK.

SIBELIUS, JEAN (1865-1957)

-The Harp Player (arr. Anatol
Lybimov)
BIS LP-149
RAINER KUISMA (marimba).

SIFLER, PAUL J. (1911-   )

-Marimba Suite
For solo marimba.
WIM 5
KAREN ERVIN (marimba).

SIKORSKI, TOMASZ

-Antiphones
For soprano, magnetic tape, piano,
horn, chimes, 2 gongs, and tam-
tams.
MUZ (Muza Warsaw - Poland) 212

SILVERS/De SYLVA

-April Showers
Nexus NE-01
NEXUS.

SIMONS, NETTY (1913-   )

-Design Groups No. 1
For solo percussion.
Desto DC-7128
RON GEORGE (percussion).

-Puddintame
For two limericists and two
percussionists.
CRI SD-309
JEAN-CHARLES FRANCOIS and RON
GEORGE (percussion).

SIMPSON, DUDLEY

-Expose
For 5 timpani, 4 roto-toms,
vibraphone, tubaphone, bass
marimba, xylophone, large bass
drum, large tam-tam, 2 suspended
cymbals, and tamburo militare.
Classics For Pleasure CFP-40207
TRISTAN FRY (percussion).

SLAVICKY, MILAN (1947-   )

-The Way of the Heart
For violin, winds, celesta,
percussion, and harp.
Supraphon 1110 3398

SLAWSON, BRIAN/HALPERIN, ART

-Tricentennial
CBS Records M-39704 Stereo
BRIAN SLAWSON (keyboard
percussion).

CBS Records MK-39704 (Compact
Disc)
BRIAN SLAWSON (keyboard
percussion).

SMADBECK, PAUL

-**Etude No. 1**
-**Etude No. 2**
-**Etude No. 3**
For marimba.
Mallet Arts Inc.   M-101
PAUL SMADBECK (marimba).

-**Rhythm Song.**
For one or more marimbas.
Mallet Arts Inc.   M-101
PAUL SMADBECK (marimbas).

SMIT, LEO (1921-   )

-**In Woods**
For oboe, harp, and percussion.
Orion 79333
JAN WILLIAMS (percussion).

SMITH BRINDLE, REGINALD (1917-   )

-**Orion 42**
For 3 tom-toms, 2 timbales, timpani,
vibraphone, 2 suspended cymbals, 2
crotales, 2 triangles, castanets, 3
wood blocks, 3 temple blocks,
bamboo chimes, and tam-tam.
Classics For Pleasure CFP-40207
TRISTAN FRY (percussion).

SOLER, JOSEP

-**El Cant i com el cant de rossynol**
For vibraphone solo.
THO MTH 218
SIEGFRIED FINK (vibraphone).

-**Noche Oscura**
For organ and percussion.
CBS Sony 32DC 691 (Compact Disc)
MAKOTO ARUGA (percussion).

SOLLBERGER, HARVEY (1938-   )

-**Sunflowers (1976)**
For flute and vibraphone.
CRS 8425

New World Records NW 254
CLAIRE HELDRICH (vibraphone).

-**The 2 and the 1** (1972)
For two percussionists and cello.
New World Records NW 330
THE NEW MUSIC CONSORT.

SOLOMON, LARRY

-**Music of the Spheres**
For marimba.
Studio 4 Productions S4P-R101
KAREN ERVIN (marimba).

SONDHEIM, STEPHEN (1930-   )

-**Send in the Clowns** (arr. R. Gipson)
For percussion ensemble.
Second Hearing GS 9008
UNIVERSITY OF OKLAHOMA
PERCUSSION ENSEMBLE.

SOUSTER, TIM (1943-   )

-**Sonata**
For cello, piano, 7 winds, and
percussion.
Leonarda 114

SPIEGEL, LAURIE (1945-   )

-**Drums**
Capriccio 2

SPIVACK, LARRY

-**Soliloquy**
For vibraphone.
Lang Percussion Company - New
York (Cassette only)
LARRY SPIVACK (vibraphone).

STABILE, JAMES

-**Ballade** (arr. Theodore Frazeur)
Instructional Resources Center APD
075S
THE FREDONIA PERCUSSION
ENSEMBLE. Theodore C. Frazeur,
director.

STARER, ROBERT (1924-   )

-**Concerto for viola, strings, and percussion**
Turnabout 34692

STEIN, LARRY   See also: **BERGAMO, JOHN**

-Elementary Junk
Robey Records ROB. 1
REPERCUSSION UNIT.

-It's Ridiculous
CMP Records CMP 31 CS
REPERCUSSION UNIT

-L.A.
Robey Records ROB. 1
REPERCUSSION UNIT.

-Orfacape
CMP Records CMP 31 CS
REPERCUSSION UNIT

-Plane Story. The
CMP Records CMP 31 CS
REPERCUSSION UNIT

-Spring Song
Robey Records ROB. 1
REPERCUSSION UNIT.

STEIN, LEO (1910-   )

-Introduction and Rondo (1960)
For flute and percussion.
CRS 8425
TAMBOUS DUO.

STEINER, GITTA (1932-   )

-Concert Piece for Seven No. 1
For cello, flute, piccolo, piano, voice,
and percussion.
Instructional Resources Center APD
075S
MARGARET MALONE and DENISE
DOMRES (percussion).

STIBILJ, MILAN (1929-   )

-Epervier de ta Faiblesse. Domine
Philips Stereo 836.991 DSY
LES PERCUSSIONS DE STRASBOURG.

-Hystus
For percussion and orchestra.
RTV Ljubljana LD 0707

-Zoom
For clarinet and bongos.
RTV Ljubljana LD 0387

STOCK, DAVID (1939-   )

-Triple Play (1970)
For piccolo, bass, and percussion.
CRI SD-490
PITTSBURGH NEW MUSIC ENSEMBLE.

STOCKHAUSEN, KARLHEINZ (1928-   )

-Aufwärts (Aus den sieben tagen)
For piano, viola, trombone, 2 tam-
tams, and electronics.
DGG 2530 255
ALFRED ALINGS and ROLF GEHLHAAR
(percussion).

Harmonia Mundi 30899 M

-Aus den Sieben Tagen fuer Ensemble
For electronium, tam-tams,
percussion, piano, double bass, viola,
sax, flute, trombone, Hammond
organ, voice, short wave receiver,
glass with stones, nails, hammer,
timber, sand-paper, file, rasp, 4 car
horns, siren whistle, 2 rin, 2 filters,
potentiometers, and sound direction.
DGG 2720 073
ALFRED ALINGS, ROLF GEHLHAAR,
and JEAN-PIERRE DROUET
(percussion).

-Auszug
SCHW HL 00 212 (5 LP's)
LES PERCUSSIONS DE STRASBOURG.

-Es (Aus den Sieben Tagen)
DG 2530 225
ALFRED ALINGS and ROLF GEHLHAAR
(percussion).

-Intensitaet
For viola, tam-tam,   piano, double
bass, percussion, sax, flute, nails,
ham- mer, timber, sand-paper, file,
rasp, 4 car horns, siren whistle, 2
filters, and volume control.
DGG 2530 256
ROLF GEHLHAAR, and JEAN-PIERRE
DROUET (percussion).

-**Japan - Aus den 17 Texten
Intuitiver Musik fuer Kommende
Zeiten**
For electronium, japanese wood-
blocks, percussion, electrochord,
and japanese bamboo flute.
EMI
CHRISTOPH CASKEL (percussion);
HAROLD BOJE and PETER EOETWOES
(japanese wood-blocks).

-**Kommunion**
For viola, tam-tams, piano, Hammond
organ, double bass, sax, flute, voice,
short-wave receiver, glass with
stones, filters, and volume controls.
DGG 2530 256
ALFRED ALINGS, JEAN-PIERRE
DROUET, and ROLF GEHLHAAR
(percussion).

-**Kontakte** (1960)
For piano, percussion, and
electronic sounds.
HM DMR 1013/15 (3 LP's)
CHRISTOPH CASKEL (percussion).

DG 138 811
CHRISTOPH CASKEL (percussion).

Wergo WER 60009
DAVID TUDOR (piano and
percussion) and CHRISTOPH CASKEL
(percussion).

-**Kontakte II**
Fuer Elektronische Klaenge, Klavier,
und Schlagzeug.
Candide CE 31022
CHRISTOPH CASKEL (percussion).

Vox-Can MM 1104

-**Kreuzspiel**
For oboe, bass clarinet, piano, and 3
percussionists.
DGG 2530 443 PSI

-**Kurzwellen fuer 6 Spieler** (1968)
For tam-tam, electronium, viola,
piano, and sound-direction.
DGG 139451-52

DGG 2707 045
ALFRED ALINGS and ROLF GEHLHAAR
(percussion).

-**Mantra** (1969-70)
For 2 pianos , percussion, and
electronics.
DG 2530208 PSI

-**Mikrophonie I**
For tam-tam, 2 microphones, 2
filters, and potentiometers.
Columbia CBS 72647
ALFRED ALINGS and ALOYS
KONTARSKY (tam-tams).

Columbia MS 7355

Columbia S-77230
ALFRED ALINGS and ALOYS
KONTARSKY (tam-tams).

DGG 2530 583

-**Musik im Bauch** (1974)
For 6 percussionists and music boxes.
DG 2530913 PSI
LES PERCUSSIONS DE STRASBOURG.

-**Opus 1970**
For piano, electric viola,
electronium, tam-tam, and sound
director.
DGG 139461 SLPM
ROLF GEHLHAAR (tam-tam).

-**Percussive Trio**
For piano and 2 timpani.
DGG 2530827 PSI
JEAN BATIGNE and GEORGES VAN
GUCHT (timpani).

-**Pole-Version Elektronium und
Elektrochord**
For electronium, japanese wood-
blocks, short-wave receiver,
electrochord, and cymbale antique.
EMI 1C165-02313
HAROLD BOJE (japanese wood-blocks)
and PETER EOETWOES (cymbale
antique).

-Prozession

For tam-tam, viola, elektronium,
piano, filters, and potentiometers.
Candide CE 31001
ALFRED ALINGS and ROLF GEHLHAAR
(tam-tam).

Candide CE 31022

Columbia CBS 77230

DG 2530 582

Var./Sara. 81008

Vox-MM 1098

-Refrain (1959)

For piano, wood-blocks, celeste,
antique cymbals, vibraphone,
cowbells, and
glockenspiel.
Time S/8001
ALOYS KONTARSKY (wood-blocks and
piano), BERNHARD KONTARSKY
(celesta and antique cymbals), and
CHRISTOPH CASKEL (vibraphone,
cowbells, and glockenspiel).

-Setz Die Segel Zur Sonne

For electronium, 2 tam-tams, piano,
double bass, viola, sax, flute,
percussion, and sound direction.
Harmonia Mundi MV-30795
ALFRED ALINGS, ROLF GEHLHAAR,
and JEAN-PIERRE DROUET
(percussion).

-Unbegrenzt

For trombone, piano, Hammon
organ, double bass, percussion, sax,
flute, viola, and sound direction.
NDLFM (Nuits de la Fondation
Maeght [France])
JEAN-PIERRE DROUET (percussion).

-Verbindung

For electronium, 2 tam-tams, piano,
double bass, viola, sax, flute,
percussion, and sound direction.
Harmonia Mundi MV-30795

-Wach-Aus den 17 Texten Intuitiver Musik fuer Kommende Zeiten

For electronium, percussion,
electrochord, and japanese bamboo
flute.
EMI 1C165-02314

-Zyklus No. 9 (1959)

For one percussionist.
Classics For Pleasure CFP 40207
TRISTAN FRY (percussion).

Columbia MS-7139
MAX NEUHAUS (percussion).

Erato R32E-1018 (Compact Disc)
SYLVIO GUALDA (percussion).

RCA Japan RDC 1
SUMIRE YOSHIHARA (percussion).

Time S/8001
CHRISTOPH CASKEL (percussion).

Wergo 60010
CHRISTOPH CASKEL and MAX
NEUHAUS (percussion).

STOUT, GORDON

-Etude No. 1
-Etude No. 2
-Etude No. 3
-Etude No. 6
-Etude No. 9
-Etude No. 11
-Etude No. 12

For marimba.
Studio 4 Productions S4P R-100
GORDON STOUT (marimba).

-Reverie

For marimba.
Studio 4 Productions S4P R-102
GORDON STOUT (marimba).

-Two Mexican Dances

For marimba.
AUD 63 407
AXEL FRIES (marimba).

Studio 4 Productions S4P R-100
GORDON STOUT (marimba).

STOUT, RICHARD

-Piece for Marimba
Studio 4 Productions S4P R-100
GORDON STOUT (marimba).

STRAESSER, JOEP (1934-   )

-Ramasasiri
For mezzo-soprano, flute, and
percussion ensemble.
Composer's Voice (Donemus Audio
Visual Series) DAVS 7475/3
THE NETHERLANDS PERCUSSION
ENSEMBLE.

STRANG, GERALD (1908-   )

-Percussion Music
For suspended symbal, 5 temple
blocks, 5 small bells, anvil, 2 wood
blocks, 3 chinese drums, triangle,
maracas, 2 gongs, and bass drum.
Orion 642
PRICE PERCUSSION ENSEMBLE.

Period Records SPL 743
PAUL PRICE, MICHAEL COLGRASS,
and WARREN SMITH (percussion).

STRAVINSKY, IGOR (1882-1971)

-Danse du Diable (from Histoire du
Soldat) (arr. John Engelman)
For 4 high, 4 medium, and 4 low
drums, 1 large bass drum, 1 small
stuffed bass drum, suspended
cymbal, and suspended iron rod.
Golden Crest CR-4016
ITHACA PERCUSSION ENSEMBLE.
Warren Benson, director.

-Histoire du Soldat (Complete).
DG 2535456 (previously issued as DG
2530609)
THE BOSTON SYMPHONY CHAMBER
PLAYERS.

-Histoire du Soldat : Suite (1918)
CBS MS-6272

CBS MS-7093

Delos DCD-3021 (Compact Disc)
LOS ANGELES CHAMBER ORCHESTRA

Delos DMS-3014 (D)
LOS ANGELES CHAMBER ORCHESTRA

Laurel 103

Quintessence 7158

RCA ARL 1-3375
Ravinia Festival Ensemble.

RCA ARL 1-3375

Reference RR-17

Reference RR-17 CD (Compact Disc)

Ultrafi 12 (Dir).

2-Vanguard T. 707/8
STOKOWSKI ENSEMBLE.

2-Vanguard 71165 (F) 10121; 71166
(E).

-Les Noces (1917-23)
Col M-33201

Nonesuch 71133

RCA ARL 1-3375
RAVINIA FESTIVAL ENSEMBLE.

SUBOTNICK, MORTON (1933-   )

-Ascent Into Air
For 2 cellos, clarinet, bass clarinet,
trombone, bass trombone, 2 pianos, 2
percussionists, and computer
generated sounds.
Nonesuch (Silver Series) 78020-1
AMY MARIE KNOLES and RAND
STEIGER (percussion).

-The Key to Songs
For 2 pianos, viola, cello, percussion,
and computer generated sounds.
New Albion NA-012
CALIFORNIA E.A.R. UNIT.

SUEYOSHI, YASUO (1937-   )

-Antigone
Fontec RFO-1040
TOMOYUKI OKADA PERCUSSION
ENSEMBLE.

-Mirage Pour Marimba
Nippon Columbia Co., Ltd. OQ-7466
KEIKO ABE (marimba).

Denon 30C0-1727 (Compact Disc)
KEIKO ABE (marimba).

Denon 35C37-7279 (Compact Disc)
KEIKO ABE (marimba).

SUKEGAWA, TOSHIYA (1930-   )

-From 5 Pieces after Paul Klee, op. 40, (In the Dim Light, One Who Runs Swiftly, Hot Points and Lines)
Denon 35C37-7279 (Compact Disc)
KEIKO ABE (marimba).

Denon 30C0-1729 (Compact Disc)
KEIKO ABE (marimba).

SYDEMAN, WILLIAM (1928-   )

-Music for flute, guitar, viola, and percussion (1962)
CRI SD-181
CONTEMPORARY CHAMBER
ENSEMBLE.

T

TAIRA, YOSHIHISA (1938-   )

-Convergence I Pour Marimba Solo
Nippon Columbia Co., Ltd. OQ-7466
KEIKO ABE (marimba).

Denon 30C0-1727 (Compact Disc)
KEIKO ABE (marimba).

Denon 35C37-7279 (Compact Disc)
KEIKO ABE (marimba).

HemisFerio Co.,   Spain (Seesaw Music
Corp., distributor - New York)
XAVIER JOAQUIN (marimba).

-Hierophonie II (1974)
For percussion sextet.
BIS LP-232 (D)
KROUMATA PERCUSSION ENSEMBLE.

BIS CD-232 (compact disc)
KROUMATA PERCUSSION ENSEMBLE.

Fontec RFO-1040
TOMOYUKI OKADA PERCUSSION
ENSEMBLE.

-Pentalpha
For five instruments.
Denon 38C37-7280 (Compact Disc)
KEIKO ABE (marimba); MAKOTO
ARUGA (percussion) (THE TOKYO
QUINTET).

TAKAHASHI, YUJI

-Nozuchi no uta
For percussion.
CBS Sony 32DC-1009 (Compact Disc)
SUMIRE YOSHIHARA (percussion).

TAKEMITSU, TORU (1930-   )

-Gitimalya
Digital JVC SJX-9567 (Japan)
MICHIKO TAKAHASHI (marimba).

-Munari by Munari (1967)
DG 2530 532
STOMU YAMASH'TA (percussion).

Rca RDCE-9
SUMIRE YOSHIHARA (percussion).

-Rain Tree
For three percussionists.
CBS Sony 32 DC 673 (Compact Disc)
SUMIRE YOSHIHARA, YASUNORI
YAMAGUCHI, ATSUSHI SUGAHARA
(percussion).

-Sacrifice
For alto flute, lute, and vibraphone.
DG 2530 088
KEIKO ABE (vibraphone).

-Seasons
L'Oiseau-Lyre DSLO 1
STOMU YAMASH'TA (percussion).

-Stanza No. 1
For mezzo-soprano, guitar, harp,
vibraphone, celesta, and piano.
DG 2530 088
KEIKO ABE (vibraphone).

TANAKA, TOSHIMITSU (1930-   )

-Two Movements for Marimba
Denon 30C0-1728 (Compact Disc)
KEIKO ABE (marimba).

TANNER, PETER (1936-   )

-Diversions
For flute and marimba.
Grenadilla 1042
TED FRAZEUR (marimba).

TANULMANY, NEGY

-4 Studies (1975)
For four percussionists.
Hungaroton SLPX 12368
ISTVAN TÜRK, SANDOR GODAN,
TÜNDE MAGDA, ZOLTAN RACZ
(percussion).

TASHJIAN, CHARMAIN (1950-   )

-Resan (1978)
For English horn, double bass, viola,
harpsichord, and percussion
instruments.
Capriccio 1
MacDONALD ENSEMBLE.

TCHAIKOVSKY, PETER I. (1840-1893)

-Serenade for Strings, Op. 48 (1st. movement)
Mark Records MES 38080
THE 1978 P.A.S.I.C MARIMBA
ORCHESTRA.

TELEMANN, GEORG PHILIPP (1681-1767)

-Canonic Sonata in A Major
Epic P-17808
VIDA CHENOWETH (marimba).

THÄRICHEN, WERNER (1921-   )

-Concerto for Timpani and Orchestra, Op. 34 (Paukenkonzert) (1954)
SCHW VMS 2066
WERNER THÄRICHEN (timpani).

Schwann Musica Mundi CD-11066
(Compact Disc)
WERNER THÄRICHEN (timpani).

THOMAS, ANDREW (1939-   )

-Roman de Fauvel
For soprano, percussion, and piano.
Opus One 8
CLAIRE HELDRICH (percussion).

THOMAS, CARTER (1950-   )

-Auric Light (1972)
For electronically modified harp and
percussion.
Press P-5001

THOMSON, VIRGIL (1896-   )

-Autum (Concertino for Harp, Strings, and Percussion)
Angel S-37300

Angel CDC-47715
LOS ANGELES CHAMBER ORCHESTRA.

-Concerto for flute, strings, and percussion
Louisville S-663

-Mass for Two-Part Chorus and Percussion
Cambridge Records CRS-412
LLOYD McCAUSLAND (percussion).

THORNE, FRANCIS (1922-   )

-Lyric Variations II (1972)
For wind quintet and percussion.
Serenus 12058
RICHARD FITZ (percussion).

-Simultaneitis (1971)
For brass quintet, electric guitar,
and percussion.
Ser. 12035

TIEFENBOCK, ALFONS (1903-1957)

-Vibraphon-Rhythmen
For vibraphone and piano.
SP 10 019
RETO PAROLARI (percussion).

TIMM, KENNETH (1934-   )

-The Joiner and the Die-Hard (1972)
For percussion.
Crystal 531
DONALD ERB (percussion).

TOENSING, RICHARD (1940-   )

-Sounds and Changes II, III, IV
(1966-79)
For organ and percussion.
Owl 27
JOHN GALM (percussion).

TOMASI, HENRI (1901-1971)

-Le Tombeau de Mireille
For soprano sax and tambourine.
Golden Crest 4206 (D)
JOE GOEBEL (tambourine).

TRADITIONAL AFRICAN MUSIC

-(No names given)
Hungaroton HCD 12855 (Compact Disc)
AMADINDA PERCUSSION GROUP.

Hungaroton SLPD 12800
AMADINDA PERCUSSION GROUP.

TRADITIONAL FIDDLE TUNE

-Rêve du Diable (Devil's Dream)
Croissant CRO-2001
REPERCUSSION.

TRUAX, BARRY

-Nautilus
For solo percussion and four
computer-synthesized sound tracks.
Melb (Melbourne [Canada]) SMLP
4033
RUSSELL HARTENBERGER
(percussion).

TSUBONOH, KATSUHIRO (1947-   )

-Meniscus
For marimba.
Denon 30C0-1729 (Compact Disc)
KEIKO ABE (marimba).

Denon 35C37-7279 (Compact Disc)
KEIKO ABE (marimba).

-Ripple of the Wind. (Concerto for
five players).
Denon 38C37-7280 (Compact Disc)
KEIKO ABE (marimba); MAKOTO
ARUGA (percussion) (THE TOKYO
QUINTET).

U

UDOW, MICHAEL (1949-   )

-A Bird Whispered, "Your Children Are
Dying."
University of Michigan SM-0019
UNIVERSITY OF MICHIGAN
PERCUSSION ENSEMBLE. Michael
Udow, director.

-Bog Music
University of Michigan SM-0019
UNIVERSITY OF MICHIGAN
PERCUSSION ENSEMBLE. Michael
Udow, director.

-Dancing Hands
TR^2 001
MICHAEL UDOW (percussion)
with THE TONE ROAD RAMBLERS.

-Rock Etude #7 (In cooperation with
Bill Douglas)
University of Michigan SM-0019
UNIVERSITY OF MICHIGAN
PERCUSSION ENSEMBLE. Michael
Udow, director.

-Strike (1979)
Opus One 80/81
THE PERCUSSION GROUP - CINCINNATI.

-Timbrack Quartet
University of Michigan SM-0019
UNIVERSITY OF MICHIGAN
PERCUSSION ENSEMBLE. Michael
Udow, director.

V

VAN De VATE, NANCY (1930-   )

-Music for Viola, Percussion, and
Piano (1976)
Orion 80386

VAN HAUWE, WALTER See: **ABE, KEIKO**
and **JAPANESE FOLK SONG**

VAN VACTOR, DAVID (1906-   )

-Economy Band (1968)
For trumpet, trombone, and
percussion.
Golden Crest S-4085

VAN VLIJMEN, JAN (1935-   )

**-Gruppi per 20 strumenti e
percussione**
DAVS 6404

VARESE, EDGAR (1883-1965)

-Déserts (1954; rev. 1961)
For winds, percussion, piano, and
magnetic tape.
Angel S-36786

CBS M-39053
ENSEMBLE INTERCONTEMPORAIN.
Pierre Boulez, conductor.

2 CBS MG-31078

COL BRG 72106

COL ML 5762

COL MS-6362

COL SERG 72106

CRI SD-268
GROUP FOR CONTEMPORARY MUSIC
AT COLUMBIA UNIVERSITY

EMI C 061.10075

-Hyperprism (1922-23)
For winds and percussion.
Candide 31028
"DIE REIHE" ENSEMBLE.

CBS M-39053
ENSEMBLE INTERCONTEMPORAIN.
Pierre Boulez, conductor.

2-CBS MG-31078

-Intégrales (1924-25)
For 11 winds and 4 percussionists.
Candide 31028
"DIE REIHE" ENSEMBLE.

CBS M-39053
ENSEMBLE INTERCONTEMPORAIN.
Pierre Boulez, conductor.

2 CBS MG-31078

EMS 401
JUILLIARD PERCUSSION ORCHESTRA.

Finnadar 9018
JUILLIARD PERCUSSION ORCHESTRA.

London 41470-1 LE (previously
issued as Lon. 6752)
MEMBERS OF THE LOS ANGELES
PHILHARMONIC. Zubin Mehta,
conductor.

Nonesuch 71269
CONTEMPORARY CHAMBER
ENSEMBLE.

-Ionisation (1929-31)
For percussion instruments and
piano.
Cambridge Records 2824
THE AARHUS CONSERVATORY
PERCUSSION ENSEMBLE.

Candide 31028
"DIE REIHE" ENSEMBLE.

CBS MS-6146

2 CBS MG-31078

EMS 401
JUILLIARD PERCUSSION ORCHESTRA.

Finnadar 9018
JUILLIARD PERCUSSION ORCHESTRA.

IRC APD 075 S
THE FREDONIA PERCUSSION
ENSEMBLE. TheodoreFrazeur,
director.

London 41470-1 LE (previously
issued as Lon. 6752)

MMG 105 (D)
THE LONDON PERCUSSION ENSEMBLE.

Nonesuch H-71291
NEW JERSEY PERCUSSION ENSEMBLE.
Raymond DesRoches, director.

Elektra/Nonesuch 9 79150-2 (Compact
Disc)
NEW JERSEY PERCUSSION ENSEMBLE.
Raymond DesRoches, director.

Orion 7150

Phillips Stereo 6718 040
LES PERCUSSIONS DE STRASBOURG.

Phillips 32 CD 3063 (Compact Disc)
LES PERCUSSIONS DE STRASBOURG.

Urania UX-106
AMERICAN PERCUSSION SOCIETY.

VERCOE, ELIZABETH (1941-   )

-Herstory II. (13 Japanese Lyrics) (1979)
For soprano, piano, and percussion.
Northeastern Records North-221
BOSTON MUSICA VIVA.

VIOLETTE, ANDRE

-Black Tea
For soprano, harp, contrabass, and
percussion.
Opus One 53

VIVALDI, ANTONIO (1678-1741)

-Adagio (From Concerto in D minor for strings and continuo ["Concerto Madrigalesco"] F. XI, No. 10)
CBS Records M39704 Stereo
BRIAN SLAWSON (keyboard
percussion).

-The Four Seasons. Op.8, Nos.1-4
For five marimbas.
Firebird K33Y 141 (Compact Disc)
TOKYO MARIMBA BAND. Makoto
Aruga, conductor.

-Winter (From The Four Seasons)
CBS Records M39704 Stereo
BRIAN SLAWSON (keyboard
percussion).

W

WAGENAAR, DIDERICK (1946-   )

-Tam Tam (1978-1979)
For 2 pan flutes, 2 alto saxophones, 4
pianos, 2 bass guitars, 2 congas, and
marimba.
Composers' Voice (Donemus Audio
Visual Series) 8101
PAUL KOEK and LUUK NAGTEGAAL
(congas and marimba).

-The Shipwreck
For soprano, tenor, bass, mixed
chorus, piano, percussion, and storm
instruments.
Editio Laran ST 7073
CEES VAN STEYN and NICK WOUD
(percussion).

WALTON, (Sir) WILLIAM (1902-1983)

-Facade (1922-)
For flute, piccolo, clarinet, bass
clarinet, alto saxophone in E^b,
trumpet, cello, percussion, and
reciter.
Candide 31116

Reference RR-16
CHICAGO PRO MUSICA (original
chamber ensemble version, but
without recitation.)

Reference RR-16CD (Compact Disc)
CHICAGO PRO MUSICA (original
chamber ensemble version, but
without recitation.)

Odyssey Y-32359

WATANABE, URATO (1909-   )

**-Fantasy on ancient Japan "Yamato"
(1970)**
For xylophone and orchestra.
Japan Federation of Composers JFC-
7007
YUKIKO TAKAHASHI (marimba).
With the Symphony Orchestra of the
Japan Folk Music Association,
Chiyuki Murakata, conductor.

WATSON, WALTER (1933-   )

-Recital Suite
For marimba and piano.
Crystal S-532
KENNETH WATSON (marimba).

WAKMAN, FRANZ (1906-1962)

-Sinfonietta
For strings and timpani.
Varese/Sarabande   81052

WEBER, REINHOLD (1927-   )

-Musik fur Schlagzeug
SST 0 164
BADISCHEN CONSERVATORY
PERCUSSION ENSEMBLE.

WEHDING, HANS HENDRICK

-Concertino
Fuer elektronische Klaenge,
Streichorchester, und Schlagzeug.
Eterna (G.D.R.) 720205

WEINBERGER, JAROMIR (1896-1967)

**-Concerto for Timpani and Brass
Instruments**
Digital MD+G G1076 (West Germany)
ARNDT JOOSTEN (timpani).

WEISS, HARALD

-Schlagzeug-Werkstatt
Wergo WER T 207
HARALD WEISS (percussion).

WERNICK, RICHARD (1934-   )

-A Prayer for Jerusalem
For mezzo-soprano and percussion.
CRI S-344
GLEN STEELE (percussion).

WHEATLEY, DAVID

-Duo for Two Marimbas
Studio 4 Productions S4P R-102
GORDON STOUT and KAREN ERVIN
(marimbas).

WIDDOES, LAWRENCE (1932-   )

-Acanthus (1972)
For harp and vibraphone.
CRI S-480
DANIEL DRUCKMAN (vibraphone).

WILDER, ALEC (1907-1980)

-Sextet
For marimba and wind quintet.
Golden Crest 4190
GORDON STOUT (marimba).

Suite for Flute and Marimba (1977)
Golden Crest 4190
GORDON STOUT (marimba).

Pantheon 2031
CHRISTOPHER NORTON (marimba).

-Suite for Solo Guitar (arr. **Gordon
Stout)**
Studio 4 Productions S4P R-100
GORDON STOUT (marimba).

**-Suite for Trumpet and Marimba
(1977)**
Golden Crest 4190
GORDON STOUT (marimba).

WILLIAMS, CLIFTON (1923-1976)

-Concertino
For percussion and band.
Austin Recording Company CS-33-
6164
ROGER STALEY, JOE PULLIS, FRED
CLOSE, JOHN LOCHABY, NANCY
STEPHENSON, and ALMA GRACE
RUTHER (percussion).

WILLIAMS, J. KENT

-**African Sketches** (1968)
Cal CAL 30 492
WURZBURG MUSIC SCHOOL
PERCUSSION ENSEMBLE. Siegfried
Fink, conductor.

WILLIAMS, JAN

-**Dream Lesson**
For percussion.
Turnabout 34514
JAN WILLIAMS (percussion).

WILLIAMS, PAUL

-**Evergreen** (arr. Gipson)
Second Hearing GS 9008 (Compact
Disc)
UNIVERSITY OF OKLAHOMA
PERCUSSION ENSEMBLE.

WILSON, EUGENE (1937-)

-**The Light Fantastic Too**
For soprano, flute, piano, and
percussion.
Opus One 46

WOLFF, CHRISTIAN (1934-)

-**For 1, 2, or 3 People** (1964)
Opus One 80/81
THE PERCUSSION GROUP -
CINCINNATI.

WOLPE, STEFAN (1902-1972)

-**Piece for Trumpet and 7
Instruments**
Crystal S-352
KRAFT ENSEMBLE.

WOZNIAK, FRANCISZEK (1932-)

-**Symphony for Percussion**
MUZA SXL 0809

-**Quartet**
For tenor sax, trumpet, piano, and
percussion.
Nonesuch 71302
RAYMOND DesROCHES (percussion).

WUORINEN, CHARLES (1938-)

-**Arabia Felix**
For flute, bassoon, guitar, violin,
vibraphone, and piano.
CRI S-463
CONTEMPORARY MUSIC GROUP.

-**Janissary Music** (1966)
For solo percussion.
CRI S-231
RAYMOND DesROCHES (percussion).

-**Percussion Duo** (1979)
For percussion and piano.
CRI SD-459
STEVEN SCHICK (percussion).

-**Percussion Symphony** (1976)
Nonesuch H-71353
NEW JERSEY PERCUSSION ENSEMBLE.
Charles Wuorinen, conductor.

Elektra/Nonesuch 9 79150-2
(Compact Disc)
NEW JERSEY PERCUSSION ENSEMBLE.
Charles Wuorinen, conductor.

-**Prelude and Fugue**
Golden Crest CR 4004

-**Ringing Changes** (1969-1970)
For percussion ensemble.
Nonesuch H-71263
NEW JERSEY PERCUSSION ENSEMBLE.
Charles Wuorinen, conductor.

-**Spinoff** (1983)
For violin, double bass, and conga
drums.
Bridge 2005

-**Variations for Bassoon, Harp, and
Timpani** (1972)
New World Records 209
GORDON GOTTLIEB (timpani).

WYATT, SCOTT A. (1951-)

-**Two Plus Two** (1975)
For percussion and tape.
UBRES CS-303 Stereo
TOM SIWE and DON BAKER
(percussion).

X

XENAKIS, IANNIS (1922-   )

-Persephassa
Philips Stereo 6718 040
LES PERCUSSIONS DE STRASBOURG.

-Pleiades
For six percussionists.
CBS Sony 32DC 691 (Compact Disc)
MAKOTO ARUGA PERCUSSION
ENSEMBLE. Makoto Aruga, conductor.

-Psappha (1975)
For percussion instruments.
BIS LP-256
GERT MORTENSEN (percussion).

CBS Sony 32 DC 673 (Compact Disc)
SUMIRE YOSHIHARA (percussion).

Erato R32E-1019 (Compact Disc)
SYLVIO GUALDA (percussion).

Erato STU-71106
SYLVIO GUALDA (percussion).

HemisFerio Co., Spain (Seesaw Music
Corp., distributor - New York).
XAVIER JOAQUIN (percussion).

Y

YAMASH'TA, STOMU (1947-   )

-Sea and Sky
Kuckuck LP-072

Kuckuck CD-072 (Compact Disc)

YOSHIHARA, SUMIRE

-Umenonaka (In the Dream)
CBS Sony 32 DC 673 (Compact Disc)
SUMIRE YOSHIHARA (percussion).

YOSHIOKA, TAKAYOSHI

-Paradox III (1978)
Opus One 80/81
THE PERCUSSION GROUP - CINCINNATI.

YOSHIZAKI, KIYOTOMI (1940-   )

-Cabala
For marimba.
CBS Sony 32 DC 5027 (Compact Disc)
MICHIKO TAKAHASHI (marimba).

-In Time of the Disorderly Palace
For percussion.
Japan Federation of Composers JFC-
8110
KEIZO KODAMI, ICHIRO HOSOYA,
MASAMI TACHIBANA, TOMO-O ONO,
IKUMO KONDO (percussion).

YUASA, JOYI (1929-   )

-Sousokusouniyu II
For percussion.
CBS Sony 32 DC 673 (Compact Disc)
SUMIRE YOSHIHARA (percussion).

-Territory
For marimba, flute, clarinet,
contrabass, and percussion.
Denon 38C37-7280 (Compact Disc)
KEIKO ABE (marimba); MAKOTO
ARUGA (percussion) (THE TOKYO
QUINTET).

YUYAMA, AKIRA (1932-   )

-Divertimento
For marimba and alto saxophone.
Denon 30C0-1728 (Compact Disc)
KEIKO ABE (marimba).

Mallet Arts Inc. M-101
PAUL SMADBECK (marimba).

Z

ZAIMONT, JUDITH LANG (1945-   )

-The Magic World (1979)
For baritone, piano, and percussion.
Leonarda 116.

ZIFFRIN, MARYLIN JANE (1926-   )

-Trio (1973)
For xylophone, soprano, and tuba.
Capra 1210
DEAN ANDERSON (xylophone).

ZONN, PAUL (1938-   )

-Divertimento No. 1
For tuba, double bass,   and 2
percussionists.
UBRES 101

ZUMBACH, ANDRE

-Cris
Pour baryton-recitant, flute,
percussion, et bande magnetique.
CTS 44
YVES HERWAN (percussion).

Directory of Record Companies and Distributors

Ades:	(distr. Harmonia Mundi)
Advance:	(distr. New Music Distribution Center)
Advent:	Advent Productions P.O. Box 772 El Cerrito, CA 94530
AF:	(see: Audiofidelity)
AMU:	(distr. Mode)
Ang. (Angel):	(distr. Capitol)
Apost. (Apostrophe):	(distr. Prodisc)
ARA:	Arabesque Recordings 60 East 42nd. Street, Suite 1705 New York, NY 10165 tel. (212) 983-1414/1415
ARC:	(see: Austin Record Company)
ARCH:	1750 ARCH Records 1750 Arch Street Berekeley, CA 94709
Argo:	(distr. Polygram Classics)
Asian Sound Records:	Asian Sound c/o Michael Ranta Venloer Strasse 176 5000 Köln 30 West Germany tel (0221) 52-8775
AST:	Astrée (distr. Harmonia Mundi)
Atlantic:	75 Rockefeller Plaza New York, NY 10019 tel (212) 484-6000
Attaca:	Attacca Babel BV Haast Records 99 Prinseneiland 1013 LN Amsterdam, Netherlands

AUD:	Audat Records P.O. Box 2000 Bowmanville, Ontario L1C 3Z3 Canada
Audio Source:	Audio Source 1185 Chess Dr. Foster City, CA 94404
Audiofidelity:	Audiofidelity Enterprises Inc. 519 Capobianco Plaza Rahway, NJ 07065
Aul.(Aulos):	Aulos Schallplatten D-4060 Viersen 11 Frankfurt, Germany (distr. Koch Import Service)
Austin Record Company:	(*)
Auvidis:	(distr. Harmonia Mundi)
Avant:	(distr. Crystal) Avant Records 6331 Quebec Drive Hollywood, CA 90068
AWS(American Wind Symphony):	American Wind Symphony Orchestra P.O. Box 1824 Pittsburgh, PA 15230 tel (412) 681-8866
BIS:	(distr. Qualiton Imports)
Boston Music Company:	Boston Music Company 9 Airport Dr. Hopedale, MA 01747
Boston Records:	(*)
Bridge:	Bridge Records, Inc. Box 1864 New York, NY 10016 tel. (516) 487-1662
CAL (Calliope):	(distr. Qualiton Imports)
CAM:	(see: Camerata)
Cambridge:	Cambridge Records 125 Irving Street Framingham, MA 01701
Camerata:	Camerata Schallplatten, Moseler Verlag Hoffmann-von-Fallersleben Strasse 8 (334) Wolfenbuttel, Germany
Candide:	(distr. Moss Music Group)

Candide/Vox: (distr. Moss Music Group)

Cantate: Barenreiter   Tonkunsverlag
                                            Barenreiter Weg 6-8
                                            (35) Kassel, Germany

CAP   (see: Capitol)

CAPAC: (*)

Capitol: Capitol Records, Inc.
                                            1750 N. Vine St.
                                            Hollywood, CA 90028
                                            tel (213) 462-6252

Capra: (distr. CRS)

Capriccio (Cassettes and CD's):   (distr. Delta)

Capriccio (LP's):   7315 Hooking Rd.
                                            Mc Lean, VA 22101
Caprice: (distr. Harmonia Mundi)

CAR: Carthage Records
                                            (distr. Rounder)

CBC: CBC Enterprises
                                            Audio Products Dept.
                                            Box 6000
                                            Station A, Montreal, Quebec
                                            Canada H3C 3A8
                                            tel (514) 285-4040
                                            (U.S. distribution by Intercon)

CBS: CBS Records Inc.
                                            51 W. 52nd St.
                                            New York, NY 10019
                                            tel (212) 975-4321

CBS Special Products: 51 W. 52nd St.
                                            New York, NY 10019
                                            tel (212) 975-5073

*CCM (Contemporary Canadian
    Music):*   Canadian Music Centre
                                            1263 Bay St.
                                            Toronto, Ontario
                                            Canada M5R 2G1

CDM: Chant du Monde
                                            24-32 Rue des Amandiers
                                            Paris, France   75020

Celestial Harmonies: 605 Ridgefield Rd.
                                            Wilton, CT 06897
                                            tel (203) 762-0558

Centrediscs: (distr. CCM)

CFP *(Classics for Pleasure):*   (part of EMI/distr. Capitol)

Charlin: (distr. Qualiton Imports)

CHR *(Christophorous):*   Christophorous Verlag Herder GmbH.
                                         Hermann-Herder-Strasse 4, 7800
                                         Freiburg, Germany
                                         (distr. Koch Import Service)

Classic Performances: (*)

CMP: (see: Creative Music Productions)

CMS: CMS Records, Inc.
                                         226 Washington St.
                                         Mount Vernon, NY 10553
                                         tel (914) 667-6200

Colo: (*)

Columbia: (distr. CBS)

Composers Recordings Inc.:   Composers Recordings Inc.

Composers' Voice (DAVS):   (see: DAVS)

Conservatory: (*)

Consortium: Consortium
                                         2451 Nichols Canyon
                                         Los Angeles, CA 90046

Contemporary Record Society: Contemporary Record Society
                                         724 Winchester Rd.
                                         Broomall, PA 19008

Cornell University (Cornell U):   Lincoln Hall
                                         Ithaca, NY 14850

Coro. (Coronet):   4971 N. High St.
                                         Columbus, OH 43214

CPR: Capri Records
                                         2008 Cotner Ave., Suite 2
                                         Denver, CO 80210

CP2:   CP2 Recordings
                                         Musical Observations Inc.
                                         45 W. 60th St.
                                         New York, NY 10023

Creative Music Productions: CMP Records
                                         P.O.Box 1129
                                         5166 Kreuzau
                                         F.R. Germany
                                         (distr. Rounder)

CRI: (see: Composers Recordings Inc.)

Croissant: (see Repercussion, Inc.)

CRS: (see: Contemporary Record Society)

Crys. (Crystal):   2235 Willida Lane
                                    Sedro Wooley, WA 98284
                                    tel (206) 856-4779

CSP: (see: CBS Special Products)

CTS: (*)

DAVS: Donemus Audio Visual Series
                                    Paulus Potterstraat 14
                                    1071 CZ. Amsterdam, Holland

Delos: Delos Records, Inc.
                                    2210 Wilshire Blvd., Suite 664
                                    Santa Monica, CA 90403
                                    tel (213) 459-7946

Delta: Delta Music Inc.
                                    2008 Cotner Ave., Suite 2
                                    Los Angeles, CA 90025
                                    tel (213) 479-0667

Denon: (LP's) (distr. Audio Source)
                                    (CD's and Cassettes) distr.:
                                    Denon America Inc.
                                    222 New Road
                                    Parsippany, NJ 07054
                                    tel (201) 575-7810

Desto: (distr. CMS)

DG (Deutsche Grammophon):   (distr. Polygram Classics)

DGG (Deutsche Grammophon
    Gesellschaft):   (distr. Polygram Classics)

Disco Center: Disco Center Vereinigte Schallplatten
                                    Vertriebsges, Postfach 10 1029
                                    (3500) Kassel, Germany

ECM/Warner Brothers: (distr. Polygram Records)

Editio Laran: (*)

Editions Orphée Inc.:   Editions Orphée Inc.
                                    P.O. Box 21291
                                    Columbus, OH 43221
                                    tel (614) 457-7609

Elect. (Electrecord):   Electrecord Recording 60
                                    Str. Luigi Cazzavillan 14-16
                                    Bucharest, Rumania

Elektra:	Elektra/Asylum/Nonesuch Records 75 Rockefeller Plaza New York, NY 10019
Elektra Nonesuch:	(distr. Elektra)
EMI (EMI America):	(distr. Capitol)
EMS:	(*)
Epic:	(distr. CBS)
Erato:	(distr. RCA)
ESP-DISK:	ESP-DISK Records P.O. Box 46 New York, NY 10018
Eterna:	Eterna Schallplatten Leipziger Str. 26 Berlin 102, East Germany
Everest:	Everest Records 2020 Ave. of the Stars Century City, CA 90067
Fin. (Finlandia):	(distr. Harmonia Mundi)
Finnadar:	(distr. Atlantic)
Folk. (Folkways):	Folkways 632 Broadway New York, NY 10012
Fontec:	(Inquire at JFC)
FSM (FSM/Pantheon):	(distr. Pantheon)
GAIA Records):	GAIA Records, Ltd. 260 West Broadway New York, NY tel (212) 226-7057 (also distr. Polygram Records)
Gallo:	(distr. Qualiton Imports)
GC (Golden Crest):	Golden Crest Recordings White Horse Pike Ancora, NJ 08037 tel (609) 561-5250
Grama. (Gramavision):	(distr. GAIA Records)
Grenadilla:	Grenadilla Productions 217 E. 85th St., Suite 263 New York, NY 10028 tel (212) 628-4585 (also distr. Crystal)

Harmonia Mundi:	Harmonia Mundi USA 3364 South Robertson Blvd. Los Angeles, CA 90034 tel (213) 559-0802
Heliodor:	(part of DG/distr. Polygram Classics)
HemisFerio Co.:	(*)
HM:	(see: Harmonia Mundi)
Hung. (Hungaroton):	(distr. Qualiton Imports)
Icon:	Icon 57 Greene St. New York, NY 10012
Ina:	Institut National de l'Audiovisuel 116 Avenue du Président Kennedy Paris, France 75016
India Navig. (India Navigation):	India Navigation 177 Franklin St. New York, NY 10013
Intercon:	Intercon Music Corp. 6600 River Rd. West New York, NJ 07093 tel (201) 868-6400
International Book and Record Distributors:	International Book and Record Distributors 40-11- 24th St. Long Island City, NY 11101 tel (718) 786-2966
Intersound:	Intersound Inc. 14025 23rd Ave. North Minneapolis, MN 55441 tel (612) 559-4166
IRC (Instructional Resources Center):	(*)
IS (Intersound Munchen):	(*) (inquire at Intersound)
Japan Federation of Composers:	(see JFC)
JFC:	Japan Federation of Composers Shinanomachi Bldg. 602 33-Shinanomachi Shinjuku-ku, Tokyo Japan
JVC (JVC/Melodiya):	(distr. Moss Music Group)

Koch Import Service: Koch Import Service
95 Eads St.
West Babylon, NY 11704
tel (516) 752-0770

Kuckuck: (distr. Celestial Harmonies)

Ladyslipper: Ladyslipper Inc.
Box 3124
Durham, NC 27705
tel (919) 683-1570

Lang Percussion Company: Lang Percussion Company
633 Broadway
New York, NY 10012

Laurel: (distr. Consortium)

Leonarda: Leonarda Productions, Inc.
Box 124 Radio City Sta.
New York, NY 10019

Limelight: Mercury Recording Corp.
35 East Wacker Dr.
Chicago, IL 60601

L'Oisseau Lyre: Decca House
9 Albert Embankment
London SE1 7SW
England
(also distr. Polygram Clasiccs)

London: (distr. Polygram Classics)

Lou. (Louisville):   First Edition Records
609 W. Main St.
Louisville, KY 40202

Lovely (Lovely Music):   Lovely Music, Lt.
325 Spring St.
New York, NY 10013
tel (212) 243- 6153

Lumina: (*)

Lyr. (Lyrichord):   Lyrichord
141 Perry St.
New York, NY 10014

Mainstream: (inactive)

Mallet Arts, Inc.:   Mallet Arts, Inc.
34 South Goodman St. Room 405
Rochester, NY, 14607

Marimba Productions:	Marimba Productions P.O. Box 467 Ausbury Park, NJ 07712 tel (201) 774-0088
Mark Records:	Mark Educational Recordings 10815 Bodine Rd. Clarence, NY 14031
Marus:	Marus Schallplatten Joachim-Friedrich-Str. 55 1000 Berlin 31 West Germany
Mass Art:	(*)
MD + G (Musikproduktion *Dabringhaus und Grimm):*	(distr. Koch Import Service)
Melb. (Melbourne):	London Records of Canada Ltd. P.O. Box 651 Peterborough, Ontario Canada
Mer. (Mercury):	(distr. Polygram)
Mercury (Golden Imports):	(distr. Polygram)
MGE:	MGE Recordings Canadian Music Centre 1263 Bay Street, Toronto Ontario, Canada M5R 2C1
MGM:	MGM Records 7165 Sunset Blvd. Hollywood, CA 90046
MHS:	(see: Musical Heritage Society, Inc.)
MMG:	(see: Moss Music Group)
Mode:	Mode Records Box 375 Kew Gardens, NY 11415 tel (718) 297-0716 (also distr. Harmonia Mundi)
Moss Music Group:	200 Varick St. New York, NY 10014 tel (212) 243-4800
MRS:	(see: Marus)
MTV:	Ministerio de Trabajo de Venezuela Caracas Venezuela
Music Gallery Editions:	(see: MGE)

Music Masters:	1710 Highway 35 Ocean, NJ 07712 (also distr. Intercon)
MUZA:	Ars Polonia P.O. Box 1001 Warzaw, Poland
NA (New Albion):	New Albion 584 Castro St. 463 San Francisco, CA 94114 tel (415) 641-5757
New Music Distribution Center:	New Music Distribution Center 500 Broadway New York, NY 10012
New World:	New World Records 701 7th Ave. New York, NY 10036
Nexus:	Nexus P.O. Box 100 Norland Ontario, Canada K0M 2L0
Nippon Columbia:	Nipon Columbia Co., Ltd. 4-14-4 Akasaka Minato-ku, Tokyo 107 Japan (see also: Denon)
Non Sequitur Records:	(*)
None. (Nonesuch):	(distr. Elektra)
North. (Northeastern Records):	Northeastern Records Box 116 Boston, MA 02117 tel (617) 437-5485
Odyssey:	(distr. CBS)
OMR:	Olympic Marimba Records and Awesome Music Productions 5521 A University Way NE Seattle, WA 98105 tel (206) 527-4989
Op. One (Opus One):	Box 604 Greenville, ME 04441
Orion:	Orion Records Box 4087 Malibu, CA 90265
Orphi. (Orphica Critica):	(*)

Outlet Book Co.:	Outlet Book Co. 225 Park Ave. South New York, NY 10003
Owl:	Owl Records Box 4536 Boulder, CO 80306
Pantheon:	(distr. Outlet Book Co.)
Paula (Paula Denmark):	(distr. Editions Orphée)
Period:	(inactive)
Phi. (Philips):	(distr. Polygram Classics)
Polskie Nagrania:	(*)
Polygram:	(see: Polygram Classics Inc.)
Polygram Classics Inc.:	Polygram Classics Inc. 810 7th Ave. New York, NY 10019 tel (212) 333-8000
Pos. (Poseidon):	(distr. Crystal)
Press:	Press Records 262 Rio Circle Decatur, GA 30030 tel (404) 377-2880
Pro. (Protone):	Protone Records 970 Bel Air Rd. Los Angeles, CA 90077 tel (213) 472-5344
Pro Viva:	Intersound GmbH Schleibingerstrasse 10 D-800 Munich 80 Federal Republic of Germany
Prodisc:	Prodisc 19 Rue de Rhinau 67100 Strasbourg France
PSAL. (Psallite):	Nordd. Tonstudio fur Kirchenmusik 3079 Warmsen 1 Bohnhorst 145 Germany
Qualiton Imports:	Qualiton Imports Ltd. 39-28 Crescent St. Long Island City, NY 11101 tel (718) 937-8515

RCA:

RCA Records
1133 Ave. of the Americas
New York, NY 10036
tel (212) 930-4000

Redw. (Redwood):

Redwood Records
6400 Hollis St.
Emeryville, CA 94608
tel (415) 428-9191

Ref. (Reference):

Reference   Recordings
Box 77225X
San Francisco, CA 94107
tel (415) 355-1892

Repercussion, Inc.:

Repercussion,   Inc.
P.O. Box 308
Place D'Armes
Montreal, P.Q. H2Y 3H1
Canada

Robbey Records:

Robbey   Records
P.O. Box 808
Newhall, CA 91322-0808

Rounder:

Rounder   Records
One Camp St.
Cambridge, MA 02140
tel (617) 354-0700

RTV:

RTV Sales Corp.
4375 SW 60th Ave.
Ft. Lauderdale, FL 33314

Schwann (Schwann Bagel
        Düsseldorf):

Verlag Schwann, Abt. Schallplaten
Postfach 7640, 4000 Düsseldorf 1
Germany

Schwann Musica Mundi:

(distr. Koch Import Service)

Second Hearing:

Second   Hearing   Records
45 Knollwood Rd.
Elmsford, NY 10523
tel (914) 347-5200

See (See/Hear Productions):

(*)

Ser. (Serenus):

(see: Boston Music Company)

S4P :

(see: Studio 4 Productions)

Shandar:

(*)

Simax:

(distr. Qualiton Imports)

Somnath Records:	Somnath 6159 Columbia Ave. St. Louis, MO 63139
Sonic (Sonic Arts):	Sonic Arts Corp. 665 Harrison St. San Francisco, CA 94107
SP:	(*)
Spectrum:	(see: Uni-Pro Recordings)
SRA:	Sister Rosalina Abejo S.F.C.C. 37950 No. 62 Fremont Blvd. Fremont, CA 94536
SST (Sound Star Tonprod.):	(distr. Rounder)
Studio 4 Productions:	Studio 4 Productions Box 266 Northridge, CA 91328J
Sup. (Supraphon):	(distr. Denon America)
SVP:	(*)
Swedish (Swedish Society Discofil):	(distr. International Book and Record)
Tel. (Teldec):	(distr. Koch Import Service)
Tho. (Thorofon):	(distr. Qualiton Imports)
Thrust Records:	(*)
Time:	(inactive)
TR^2 (Tone Road Ramblers):	Rift Records (Tone Road Ramblers) P.O. Box 663 New York, NY 10002
Turn. (Turnabout):	(distr. Moss Music Group)
U. Iowa (University of Iowa Press):	University of Iowa Press Iowa City, Iowa 52242
Ubres:	Ubres Box 2374, Sta. A Champaign, IL 61820
Ultrafi:	(*)
Umbrella:	(*)

UNAM (Universidad Nacional
  Autónoma de México):   (*)

Unicorn (Unicorn-Kanchana):   (distr. Harmonia Mundi)

Uni-Pro Recordings: Uni-Pro Recordings
                            Harriman, NY 10926
                            tel (914) 782-7888

University of Illinois: University of Illinois School of Music
                            Urbana, IL

University of Michigan: University of Michigan School of Music
                            Ann Arbor, MI 48109

Urania: (distr. Ladyslipper)

USP: (*)

Vanguard: (distr. Welk Record Group)

Var. (Varese/Sarabande):   Varese/Sarabande Records, Inc.
                            13006 Saticoy St.
                            North Hollywood, CA 91605
                            tel (213) 875-3944

Victrola: (distr. RCA)

Vox: (distr. Moss Music Group)

Vox/Candide: (distr. Moss Music Group)

Vox Cum Laude: (distr. Moss Music Group)

Welk Record Group: 1299 Ocean Ave., Suite 800
                            Santa Monica, CA 90401
                            tel (213) 870-2989

Wer. (Wergo):   (distr. Harmonia Mundi)

WIM (Western International
  Music, Inc.):   (distr. Crystal)

(*)   Address unable to be found

Index of Performers

Index of Composition Titles

About the Compiler

FERNANDO A. MEZA is Principal Percussionist, Costa Rica National Symphony Orchestra.